STRANGE TALES
from
VIRGINIA'S
MOUNTAINS

STRANGE TALES

from

VIRGINIA'S MOUNTAINS

The NORTON WOODBOOGER
THE MISSING
BEALE TREASURE
THE GHOST TOWN OF
LIGNITE
and MORE

DENVER MICHAELS

THE
History
PRESS

Published by The History Press
Charleston, SC
www.historypress.com

Front cover, left: Internet Archive; *right*: Wikimedia Commons.
Back cover, top left: Wikimedia Commons.

Unless otherwise noted, all images are courtesy of the author.

First published 2021

Manufactured in the United States

ISBN 9781467146623

Library of Congress Control Number: 2020951662

CONTENTS

ACKNOWLEDGEMENTS

First and foremost, I must thank my wife, Stefanie. She has always been my biggest supporter and number-one fan, and her belief in me has kept me going. We are empty nesters, going on a few years now, and my work on this book and other projects has made the adjustment much harder than it needed to be. But I have big plans to make it all right!

I also have to give a shout-out to my editor, Kate Jenkins, copy editor Rick Delaney and all the good folks at The History Press. I cannot thank them enough for taking a chance on me and this book. I am truly grateful for the opportunity.

INTRODUCTION

The mountains are calling and I must go.
—John Muir

What comes to mind when thinking of Virginia? Maybe you are a foodie and imagine peanuts, country ham and Brunswick stew. Perhaps you enjoy a glass of Virginia wine or a craft beer from one of the many breweries scattered throughout the state. Do you think of the terrible Sunday traffic on I-81? Are you a history buff who visits the many Civil War battlefields? Do you think of the Old Dominion as the "mother of presidents" or the national leader in vanity license plates?

For many, it is the mountains that run along Virginia's western counties that come to mind when they think of the commonwealth—and for good reason. With their stunning vistas, hundreds of miles of hiking trails, winding mountain roads, vast stretches of protected land, gorgeous waterfalls and abundance of wildlife, it is little wonder that Virginia's mountains are so beloved. This is not lost on the tourism industry; the commonwealth's official tourism website uses the slogan "Virginia is for mountain lovers" and promotes the hashtag #VAoutdoors.

These exceedingly ancient mountains, standing hard against the skyline, hold much more than rugged beauty, unparalleled recreational activities and superb animal habitat. There is also mystery, intrigue and dark secrets in these high, lonely places.

Crabtree Falls, located in the George Washington National Forest in Nelson County, is the tallest set of waterfalls in Virginia and one of the tallest east of the Mississippi River.

An amazing view from a trail in the Wolf Gap Recreation Area on the Shenandoah County, Virginia and Hardy County, West Virginia border.

A spectacular rock formation composed of hexagonal columnar basalt near Compton Peak in Shenandoah National Park.

Cascade Falls in the Jefferson National Forest in Giles County is arguably the most beautiful waterfall in Virginia. Little Stony Creek falls over a vertical cliff, and the sixty-nine-foot falls land into a pool below.

A view from atop the unique rock formation known as Dragon's Tooth in Roanoke County. The hike to Dragon's Tooth is challenging but rewarding.

The densely forested hillsides and hard-to-reach ridges conceal a resurgent mountain lion population; Bigfoot lurks here; aggressive monkeys with nasty dispositions swing through the trees and attack unsuspecting motorists; and strange flying creatures with enormous wingspans glide through the sky. And that is only for starters! An extraordinary number of UFOs crisscross Virginia airspace; nine-foot giants once ruled the land; ancient Phoenicians may have settled on isolated mountaintops; and there's gold in them hills! For those with an open mind and a love of strange stories, these mysteries and more are waiting to be explored in Virginia's mountains.

Part 1

CRYPTIDS, MONSTERS AND OUT-OF-PLACE ANIMALS

1

BIG CATS

The Wampus Cat is, according to folklore, a harbinger of death.
—*Cindy Parmiter,* True Stories of the Paranormal, *Volume 5*

WAMPUS CATS

If you grew up in the mountains and spent any length of time outdoors, at one time or another you probably heard an old-timer exclaim, "That sounds like an ole wampus cat!" in response to a growl, scream or unexplained noise in the woods. But have you ever wondered exactly what this mysterious creature of Appalachian folklore is? What is a wampus cat, and where did it come from?

The term *wampus cat* probably derived from the word *catawampus*. Although catawampus today means askew or cattycorner (at least in the South), in older times, it denoted a dreaded and unexplained creature in the woods. Perhaps the beast in question could have been more easily explained by a mountain lion, also called a catamount. Some believe that *catawampus* became mountain slang for the word *catamount*, but with all of the folklore and intrigue associated with the wampus cat, maybe there is more to it than just being a mountain lion—as frightening as mountain lions are!

Legend holds that the wampus cat has large claws and hideous fangs and is capable of walking upright. Maybe its most notable characteristic is the horrible, piercing scream it belts out in the dead of night. In the nineteenth

A cartoonish depiction of the legendary wampus cat from Henry H. Tryon's 1939 book *Fearsome Critters*. Illustration by Margaret R. Tryon. *Wikimedia Commons*.

and early twentieth centuries, wampus cats were blamed for the deaths of livestock throughout the mid- and southern Appalachians. The wampus cat, though no one really knew what it was, became a deadly, stealthy predator in the minds of mountain folks. Some say that it is simply a folkloric creature that evolved over time; some even think it bears similarities to the water panthers of Native American lore.

Perhaps the most cited wampus cat legend tells of a beautiful Cherokee woman who was cursed by her village medicine man. According to legend, the woman's husband often accompanied other men of the camp on hunting trips. Before the hunt, the men would gather in the woods for a sacred ceremony with their medicine man, seeking supernatural help and guidance on their hunt. Women were forbidden to take part in the ritual or to even see it. As the old adage goes, however, curiosity killed the cat.

One night, the woman followed her husband and the hunting party into the woods. She watched the ceremony from what she thought was a safe distance while hiding underneath the hide of a mountain lion. Unfortunately for her, the medicine man spotted her and inflicted a harsh punishment on her. He caused the skin of the mountain lion to become fused to her own until it turned into her own skin. He then doomed her to forever roam the hills alone—she became the wampus cat. Even today, she lets out eerie cries in the dead of night, and when she becomes angered at her cursed existence, she kills a pet or a livestock animal, or, if the opportunity arises, she takes the life of an unsuspecting person.

So, is this woman turned mountain lion roaming the mountains of Virginia and beyond? Probably not. But contrary to what a lot of folks will tell you, including the Virginia Department of Wildlife Resources (formerly the Virginia Department of Game and Inland Fisheries), mountain lions are.

MOUNTAIN LIONS

While these reports are popular and receive a lot of shares on social media, no big cats have been found to exist here in Virginia.
—Virginia Department of Game and Inland Fisheries

"What are you doing over there?" my wife called out.
  "I found a track!" I exclaimed.
  "What kind of track? A bear?"

"No! It's a cat track, a mountain lion has been walking around up here!"

I couldn't believe what I was seeing. I had been looking, and looking hard, for as long as I could remember for signs of mountain lions. But there it was, clear as day—no mistaking it—a track left by a big cat. It was a perfect impression in the snow that had fallen a few days earlier. I carefully looked around and found an entire series of tracks. The sizes, shapes, stride and walking pattern confirmed a mountain lion had been here a couple days earlier. I diligently photographed my finds and I even took a cast of one of the tracks. Unfortunately for me, my wife started getting a little anxious knowing a mountain lion might be nearby, so I had to leave a little earlier than I would have liked. That notwithstanding, I could not have been happier.

I had been bound and determined to find physical evidence of mountain lions since I read a statement that the Virginia Department of Game and Inland Fisheries (VDGIF) released in the fall of 2017 insisting that there were no mountain lions in Virginia. I indignantly called b——t on their statement (although I do understand, and even sympathize with, their position), because there have always been sightings in the mountains of the commonwealth, and my grandfather talked to me about them on a couple of occasions when I was in my twenties. The department's statement was in response to a fake flier that had been going around Virginia dated September 18; the flier even had the VDGIF logo printed on it. The flier warned of mountain lion sightings in the George Washington and Jefferson National Forests: "While attacks on humans are relatively rare, mountain lions can be extremely dangerous if they feel threatened." It instructed those who saw a mountain lion to notify the VDGIF and left a phone number. Additionally, it gave instructions to keep encounters as safe as possible: "Should you encounter a mountain lion, do not under any circumstances approach it and do not run away from it. Walk calmly in a safe direction and please notify the Virginia Dept. of Game and Inland Fisheries as soon as possible."

I understand the VDGIF's attempt to get out in front of the fake flier, but the line it peddles simply isn't true. Its statement confirmed that mountain lions have recently been documented as far east as Tennessee, but yet it doubled down on its position that mountain lions do not exist in Virginia.

Big cat sightings come from the far reaches of the commonwealth, from the Eastern Shore to the Cumberland Gap, all the way to the Washington, D.C. suburbs and all points in between. However, the vast majority of reports come from the mountainous regions of western Virginia. Folks visiting the George Washington and Jefferson National Forests, Shenandoah

A clear mountain lion track the author discovered in the George Washington National Forest along the Shenandoah County, Virginia and Hardy County, West Virginia line.

National Park and Blue Ridge Parkway are particularly prone to mountain lion encounters.

Bedford County is a hotbed for mountain lion sightings, and reports such as this from Deborah are quite common: "I was driving on the gravel road very near my house. A large cat came from the right side of the road and walked in front of my car—roughly thirty yards ahead. I saw it very vividly because it was not in a hurry at all. I know with certainty that it was a large cat—I estimate around seventy pounds."

In October 2017, Dena, from Bedford County, reported that her twenty-one-pound cat disappeared around the time she "saw a large cat on the edge of our mowed land and the wooded land." What struck her most was the long, thick tail of the animal. Another Bedford County resident recently saw a large cat with a "huge tail" while driving to Big Island.

Bedford County resident David had a mountain lion encounter in 2010, and in 1999, he found tracks behind his uncle's home.

> I saw one in 2010 on Goodview Road in Bedford county at 4:30 a.m. I was on my way to work and it was eating something dead on the side of the road. I saw it from a long distance as I was driving towards it, I slowed down nearly to a stop and pulled up within fifteen feet of it. It glanced at me and pounced over a fence. It was strange and so surreal but it was definitely a cougar because it had a long tail and it was huge one. I saw it clear as day right next to me. About seven miles from there in 1999, we found cougar tracks in the snow directly behind my uncle's home in Stewartsville. They were larger than my hand. I took pics of my hand next to the tracks and sent them to wildlife management. They told me that the only cougars in Virginia would be escaped pets, and potential offspring of them. Either way, they are out there.

Naturally, Shenandoah National Park with its almost two hundred thousand acres of protected land is a gold mine for mountain lion reports, which go back decades. A number of sightings were logged in the 1960s, most of which occurred along Skyline Drive. Many of the reports are similar to this 1968 sighting of a large cat, "not a bobcat, that crossed Skyline Drive and bounded up the bank and disappeared." Marylin watched a big cat cross Skyline Drive on an October morning in 1975. She said it was a light brown cat with a three- to four-foot body with small ears and a large tail. Park Rangers Rob and John described a July 1975 encounter:

> While on patrol, driving north, we observed a large yellowish-tan animal cross the road approximately one hundred feet directly in front of us (east to west). Although we only saw the animal for a brief instant, we both agreed it had all the characteristics of a puma. The animal was large: approximately sixty pounds or more, much larger than a bobcat. The animal

was cat-like in its physical structure and body movement. John T. observed a long tail and the animal was short haired. The animal was short legged, yet long in contrast to a deer or bobcat. In approximately three bounds, it crossed the road and ran up a steep embankment into the woods and rocky area. We attempted to observe it with spotlights and flashlights with no success. The following day, we returned to the area and searched for tracks but were unable to locate any, mostly due to the rocky terrain. Both of us have patrolled the "Drive" during darkness hours very frequently, and have observed many bobcats and probably all other related wildlife in the past.

Unfortunately, not all park rangers are as open to the idea of a small mountain lion population in Shenandoah National Park as Rob and John are. Diana Marchibroda found this out the hard way in 2016, when she saw a mountain lion in the park near Afton. For a period lasting at least four seconds, she watched a large, sleek cat with a long tail cross Skyline Drive.

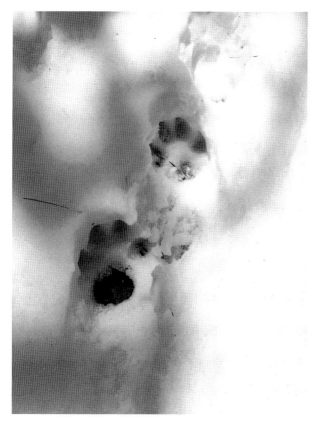

Two clear mountain lion tracks the author found near the Tibbet Knob trail in March 2018.

The author standing on McAfee Knob. According to comments in an online hiking forum, a hiker spotted a mountain lion on the trail to McAfee Knob a week prior to the author's visit.

Marchibroda, an experienced outdoorsperson, said, "I saw a mountain lion, and that's just the way it is."

Marchibroda reported her sighting to a ranger near Matthews Arm Campground and, later, to other wildlife experts, who brushed off her testimony. "They had their minds set and there was nothing that was going to change their minds. Even with all these numerous sightings they still dug their heels in, and that was pretty frustrating," she said. "They initially didn't want to admit that I saw one, and they were calling it a UFO—an unidentified furry object. I really took offense to that."

It is for this reason that I have focused much of my own time and energy toward trying to capture a big cat on camera and, better yet, on video. I have all but given up my quest to locate the "Hide and Seek Champion of the World," Bigfoot, in favor of tracking down these stealthy cats. Though mountain lions are far less sexy than Bigfoot, especially with the prevalence of cable television shows and Bigfoot Facebook groups, there is no doubt whatsoever that mountain lions exist. Moreover, Virginia lies within the historical range of mountain lions in the eastern United States. The last confirmed wild mountain lion in the commonwealth was supposedly killed in Washington County in 1882. With this in mind, looking for signs of mountain lions is a a top priority when I divvy up my spare time.

I have received a few mountain lion reports myself, one from my sister. She used to live in Bentonville, and in the winter, you could see Skyline Drive from her house. One night, while driving home, she saw a mountain lion cross the road. She claimed it was "way bigger than a bobcat, and had a long tail." Secondhand accounts have come to me from Bull Run Mountain in Prince William and Fauquier Counties. I have spoken to a couple of folks I know who live there who have been told of sightings; one even occurred on his neighbor's property. As crazy as it might sound for people to report seeing mountain lions only forty or so miles from Washington, D.C., there are many credible reports from Loudoun County, also a short drive from the Capital Beltway, especially along the border with Clarke County. There are even reports from wooded areas in Fairfax County—quite a few, in fact! Though these are much harder to believe given the population density, there are still unspoiled tracts of land in the county, and the eyewitnesses certainly believe they saw mountain lions.

BLACK PANTHERS

There is another aspect to the big cat phenomenon in the Virginia mountains: the cats are often described as being black in color. I remember, in the early nineties, my grandfather telling me about black panther sightings in Giles and Craig Counties and across the state line into West Virginia. Little did I know at the time that sightings of black panthers were that widespread. Take this sighting, by Pauline, for instance:

> *On Thursday, March 15, 2018, while driving north on the Skyline Drive in the very early afternoon, between Waynesboro (Rock Fish Gap) to Big Meadows (Byrd Visitor Center) we witnessed a large dark colored cat with a very long tail, approximately four to five feet in length, cross the Skyline Drive approximately 150 feet in front of our car. It had a very fluid and agile movement, coming out of the woods on the left, crossing the drive and going over the stone wall on the right side of the road. We were looking to spot deer and were amazed when the cat appeared in front of us. There was no one around at the time to report the sighting to, as most facilities were still closed for the season.*

A few days earlier, Lorrie and a friend saw a black panther cross U.S. 522 a mile or so south of Chester Gap (not far by the way the crow flies from Skyline Drive) in Rappahannock County. Bo spotted a big black cat while driving home from a fishing trip in western Augusta County. At first, he thought it was a bear coming out of the woods, so he pulled over so his kids and girlfriend could get a look through his binoculars. They all took turns watching the animal, which was about 120 yards away, over a period of four to five minutes. They all quickly realized it was no bear they were looking at—it was a black cat! Bo estimated that the cat weighed one hundred pounds.

The following report from McDowell, in Highland County, comes from the Cougar Quest website, which logs reports of mountain lion sightings, with a special emphasis on reports from the northern Shenandoah Valley.

> *We live close to the river on a large farm with a long driveway from the road to the house. Early in November 2005 at 5:15 PM, Lele stopped to open the gate to our driveway. When she stood up out of her car, she saw a black panther crouched 4' from her at the side of the driveway. It ran off across the street. It was about 20" high, 2 ½' body (not including the head) had a 2'–3' long tail, and was about the size of a large Lab (between 50 and 70 pounds). From then to now, she won't get out of the car to open the gate after dark—she calls and we go down to let her in.*

Accompanying the report on the website is an editorial note that reads:

> The Recorder *newspaper which serves Highland and Bath Counties published this story in their March 13, 2006 edition. From at least December 2005 through March 2006,* The Recorder *published attempts by residents of these counties to have the VDGIF and other wildlife personnel help take care of their concerns about wolves (wolfdogs/ wolf hybrids?), coyotes, bobcats, and other wildlife that was preying on human property and acting strangely. No cougars, no wolves in Virginia. But, a lot of reports and even frozen wolf "evidence." And, a lot of rabid animals—including a 32-pound bobcat that jumped into a pickup with its window rolled down and attacked 2 hunters.*

Buster said that he and a Virginia Division of Mined Land Reclamation inspector were driving east on Forest Service Road 700 around noon in the Jefferson National Forest in Wise County in February 2006 when they saw a "large dark-colored cat cross the road forty yards in front of my vehicle." He said, "It had a long slightly upturned tail and round head. It appeared to be three feet from rear end to snout, not including the tail, which appeared to be almost as long." The big cat then jumped the berm to the center of the road and then jumped to the road-cut bank. Buster and the inspector stopped where the cat left the road and got out and looked for tracks but could not find any. He said, "I am a geologist and outdoorsman and spend a lot of time in the woods, but I have never seen anything like this." He claimed what he saw was bigger than a bobcat and that it had a long tail. He said, "I have heard accounts of cougar sightings on Black Mountain and Pine Mountain from people I believe, but I always thought that a 'black panther' was a mythical folk tale."

I could continue for pages with sightings of black panthers in the mountains of Virginia, but that is not necessary. Like their tawny-colored counterparts, there is more than enough anecdotal evidence to believe that there is something to the phenomenon. However, with the black cat sightings, there is a problem. Melanism—the increased development of melanin, the dark-colored pigment in the skin and hair (the opposite of albinism)—has never been observed in mountain lions. Roughly 5 percent of jaguar populations exhibit a melanistic trait, but not so for mountain lions. So, what now?

There are too many reports—many of which are credible—to ignore, and the standard explanations that skeptics give are lacking, to say the least.

A favorite among naysayers is to blame black panther sightings on standard housecats! Yes, that is correct; skeptics argue that eyewitnesses often misjudge the size of the cat they see, and, therefore, domestic black cats are the culprit behind many encounters.

When eyewitnesses did not misjudge the size of the cat they encountered, then they probably just saw a dog—at least, according to the scoffers. A favorite fallback explanation the skeptics use is that eyewitnesses mistook their black panther sighting for a black Labrador Retriever! That is right, hardened cynics would rather believe house cats and black Labs are causing the bulk of black panther sightings than to entertain the thought that maybe, just maybe, witnesses are seeing exactly what they claim.

While it is possible that the occasional witness might (somehow) mistake a dog for a big cat, this explanation simply falls flat, in my opinion. And, once in a while, someone might misjudge the size of a house cat, especially if there is nothing in the background for scale and/or if the distance is misjudged, but this can only represent a small percentage of reports and is not a good explanation, either.

If we are going to go down the road of misidentification or misjudged size, I would suggest that fishers are much better candidates than domestic cats and black dogs. The fisher, more commonly called a fisher cat, is not a feline, but instead belongs to the mustelid (weasel) family. Fishers are closely related to martens, though they are quite a bit larger. Although fishers belong to the weasel family, they have a remarkably catlike look, especially when viewed from a distance. I recommended fishers as a possible explanation for some sightings, because they are much larger than house cats. Females reach between thirty and thirty-seven inches in length; males average around thirty-five to forty-seven inches in length. Fishers also have long, curved tails that resemble that of a mountain lion, even more so when viewed from a distance.

Fishers migrated to North America from Asia during the Pliocene. Until overtrapping took its toll, fishers thrived in the Appalachians, and Virginia is part of their historical range. In 1969, fishers were reintroduced to West Virginia when it struck a deal with New Hampshire. The Granite State gave twenty-three fishers to West Virginia in exchange for turkeys. The game department placed fishers in Tucker and Pocahontas Counties, but their numbers quickly grew, and today, a fisher can be spotted nearly anywhere in West Virginia, and they spill over into Virginia's western counties. I can personally attest to this, as I have seen a dead fisher on the side of the road along U.S. 522 in western Frederick County, and I saw one dart across

This illustration of a fisher cat was engraved by John Filmer and appeared in *The American Cyclopedia*, volume 7, in 1879. *Wikimedia Commons.*

a road and into the woods near my home in eastern Frederick County. Though I did not mistake the fishers for black panthers, this is certainly more plausible in some cases than the misidentification of house cats!

As mentioned earlier, about 5 percent of jaguars, which inhabit Central and South America, Mexico and parts of the American Southwest, are black in color. Could a few of these have made it into the commonwealth? This seems unlikely, although not entirely out of the question. Even if this has occurred, in my mind, it could only account for a minuscule number of black panther sightings in Virginia.

Along those lines, consider this report from Warren County by Rick S.:

*On July 16, 2013 about 6:30 PM in Warren County, Virginia, location 38°54'44.07" N, 78° 7'39.58" W, I sighted a large cat in the wild. This location is in Northern Virginia, in the Shenandoah Valley not far from the Appalachian Trail. It was full daylight, I was parked in my car, off the main highway facing a dirt road (Massanutten Mountain Rd near John Marshall Hwy) when a large cat came out of the dense woods and crossed the road ten yards ahead of me. The first thing I noticed was the peculiar gait short legs, long body, long tail, and chestnut color. I thought this is not a bobcat, could it be a cougar? Then it stopped and looked in my direction. I could clearly see a round face. This cat was not a cougar, and like nothing I had ever seen. Doing a little research I figured it out…a South American puma…a Jaguarundi (*Puma yagouaroundi*). I contacted the Smithsonian Conservation Biology Institute, which is in the area, to learn they do not keep this species of wild cat. It is said these big cats would not survive this far north. It may be rare, but I find sightings have been reported in the northern Appalachian region. There is no doubt I had spotted a Jaguarundi.*

What is interesting about this report is that, while jaguarundis are not native to the United States, many believe that a feral population exists in Florida. Could a few of these have made their way north—possibly escaping from traveling circuses—and maybe even established a small, breeding population? This seems unlikely, but then again, who is to say?

Whether or not the mountains of Virginia comprise a suitable habitat for jaguarundis, the cats fit the bill for many sightings. Like the fisher, jaguarundis more closely resemble a weasel than a feline. They have thin and long bodies, short legs, a small flattened head, a long tail and a sleek coat. Jaguarundis are much smaller than mountain lions; adults only reach about twenty pounds, with a length of thirty-five to fifty-five inches. Their coats come in three main colors: black, brownish-gray or red.

Personally, I believe a melanistic gene has evolved in small pockets of Appalachian mountain lions. Even though this trait has not been observed in mountain lions, as far as I know, it is not impossible, and it is the best fit for black panther sightings. Barbara Chaplin, who runs the Cougar Quest website, said the following, which hits the nail on the head:

Cougars are normally reported as tan, tawny, honey-tan, reddish-tan, greyish-tan, light brown, brown, soil-brown—all using a variety of

A photograph of a jaguarundi in captivity. Could jaguarundis be behind sightings of black panthers in Virginia? *Wikimedia Commons.*

brown. However, dark colored cougars have been reported in the Northern Shenandoah Valley and elsewhere for many years and are normally called black panthers by their observers. Most scientists believe that a melanin (black) variety is impossible; most cougar research groups immediately dismiss all reports of black-colored cougars. A very small group of scientists and only a very few cougar researchers believe that dark grey/ black cougars may be a possible color variation in small pocket populations where inbreeding from too small a resident gene pool results in physical oddities, such as the pugged faces found in the endangered Florida panther population, kinked tails, or dark (melanin) coats. On the other hand, there aren't supposed to be any cougars in the eastern states—none at all. Why then distinguish that there are no black ones if there are also no brown ones?...All observations from credible eyewitnesses are worth noting and mapping to determine clustered locations of possible cougar presence.

The statement is well said, and no greater point can be made than asking why we should differentiate between black and tan big cats, and even exclude black panther sightings? Tan-colored mountain lions are not supposed to exist in Virginia, either!

CLOSING THOUGHTS

What are we to make of the mountain lion reports and their black-colored cousins? As stated, I believe mountain lions are here, and have been here, and the black panthers are mountain lions, too. The real question to ask is, where are these cats coming from? Or, did they not die out in the first place?

While many wildlife biologists attribute confirmed mountain lion sightings to western pumas that have wandered far outside their range, some do not believe a distinction between western and eastern pumas is necessary.

Dr. Michelle LaRue commented on the matter: "I'm of the opinion that there really never was a big difference between the eastern cats and what's in existence now. I think it's all the same." Virginia Department of Game

The author found this series of mountain lion tracks near the Tibbet Knob trail in March 2018.

and Inland Fisheries district wildlife biologist David Kocka said, "I'm not a mammalogist, so I'm not going to try to play their role, but I think they're all the same." He went on to say, "There are at least ten different subspecies of white-tailed deer, and it doesn't make a bit of difference in the grand scheme of things."

I will leave any squabbling over eastern versus western pumas to those more qualified to duke it out. What I will say—and without a moment's hesitation—is that mountain lions are here. They are roaming the mountains of Virginia and beyond, and they are here to stay. It is only a matter of time before the Virginia Department of Wildlife Resources is forced to admit it.

2

BIGFOOT IN THE MOUNTAINS

The inclination to believe in the fantastic may strike some as a failure in logic, or gullibility, but it's really a gift. A world that might have Bigfoot and the Loch Ness Monster is clearly superior to one that definitely does not.
—*Chris Van Allsburg*

If you have watched news broadcasts over the last several years or paid any attention to national and, in some cases, local political campaigns, then you have heard of the controversial "sanctuary cities" throughout the nation—a hot-button issue in today's polarized political climate. But have you ever heard of a city designating itself a Bigfoot sanctuary? Probably not. But this is exactly what the city of Norton did in October 2014.

Sightings of Bigfoot, locally called Woodbooger, are common around Norton, particularly in the High Knob area. In 2011, the crew from Animal Planet's hit series *Finding Bigfoot* visited Norton and held a town hall meeting. Locals shared their Woodbooger encounters. The team also conducted a series of investigations searching for the elusive creature. Of course, they did not find Bigfoot, but their visit left a lasting impression on the town.

Partly inspired by the *Finding Bigfoot* team's visit, in 2014, the Norton City Council adopted a resolution declaring the city a Bigfoot sanctuary. The following is the text of the city council's Woodbooger resolution:

RESOLUTION   DECLARING   A   SASQUATCH/BIGFOOT
SANCTUARY
WHEREAS, The television show "Finding Bigfoot" made a stop in
Southwest Virginia in 2011 and filmed an episode concerning Bigfoot or
Sasquatch (locally known as the Woodbooger) sightings in the Norton area,
with an emphasis on the High Knob Recreation area, and
WHEREAS, if the elusive creature is as scarce and as rare as is believed
by those who seek it, and
WHEREAS, if the High Knob and adjoining City of Norton Recreational
areas are possible habitat for the creature, and
WHEREAS, if the creature is, as it appears to be, an endangered species,
NOW THEREFORE BE IT RESOLVED by the Norton City
Council, that the City of Norton is hereby declared a Sasquatch/Bigfoot/
Woodbooger sanctuary.
BE IT FURTHER RESOLVED, that the City of Norton welcomes all
those who seek to find and photograph the creature without causing injury
to it or damaging the habitat in which it may reside.
Adopted this 21st day of October, 2014.

The city's three-thousand-acre Flag Rock Recreation Area pays tribute to the Woodbooger, with a trail crossing for the big guy, large orange tracks painted on the road and a Woodbooger statue placed near the majestic Flag Rock Overlook. The attraction draws visitors from across the region and Bigfoot enthusiasts from all over.

VARIOUS REPORTS IN THE MOUNTAINS

The Norton area is certainly a hot spot for Bigfoot sightings; however, an unsuspecting person could have an encounter nearly anywhere in the mountains of Virginia. These often occur at the most inopportune time. In 2004, a Scott County bowhunter was run out the woods by foul-smelling bipedal apelike creatures throwing acorns at him. Bigfoot Field Researchers Organization (BFRO) report no. 12727 states:

> *I then saw three deer running full out down the creek bed, I heard a scream*
> *and then a loud thump. Two of the deer I saw head in another direction,*
> *but the one remained down in the vegetation thrashing around.*

Countless road trippers visit the Woodbooger statue each year for a unique selfie. It is located at the Flag Rock Overlook in Norton, Virginia.

I thought perhaps it had been wounded by another hunter, and decided to go down there and investigate. As I went down the hill to the creek bed, the wind shifted blowing right in my face, the smell what I would assume was nasty body odor, was so strong it made me feel kind of sick…an uneasy feeling kind of came over me, I got scared, I then heard what I could only describe as sticks being tapped together or up against down logs or even trees, coming from two different directions.…I then heard some type of weird scream, at that moment I decide to get the heck out of dodge. I turned back up the hillside and proceeded back up towards my tree stand. The next

Just keep following the big guy's tracks to reach the Woodbooger statue at the Flag Rock Overlook.

thing I know, a white acorn bounced off the top of my head. I dismissed it as perhaps falling from a tree, but when the next one flew by my head, I realized something was throwing objects at me. I then got really scared and decided to run, as I got a little ways away I paused to catch my breath, as

This sign alerts drivers that they have entered into the "Woodbooger Sanctuary." The trail crossing is in the city of Norton's Flag Rock Recreation Area.

> *I was resting I heard whistling and gibberish popping and clicking sounds, once again in two different directions. I heard leaves crunch and out of the corner of my I eye I saw something very big trying to blend in with the trees and bushes observing me.*

This tree, several hundred yards off a trail in the George Washington National Forest, was about two and a half inches in diameter and had a suspicious break about seven feet off the ground.

The hunter said that, before his encounter, he had noticed a foul odor in the area that he hunted, but nothing that came close to the day of his experience. He also had observed strange rock stacks in the area. This may be significant, as rock stacks are often attributed to Bigfoot activity in an area. Other possible signs include broken trees, especially when the breaks are six feet or more off the ground; trees that are bowed and pinned to the ground; and odd stacks or structures made from sticks.

A Wythe County couple purportedly saw an animal that looked like a primate jump a fence on April 10, 2019. The animal was bipedal "and covered in fur," according to the witnesses. The husband, who filed the report, said: "It jumped without using any effort at all. It then proceeded to run through the field." The creature in question stood about four feet tall, leading many to believe it was a juvenile Bigfoot. However, you have to wonder if perhaps this was an escaped chimpanzee from a private collection, circus or government facility.

Left: Sticks stacked in an odd manner such as these found by the author in the George Washington National Forest are often attributed to Bigfoot activity in an area.

Below: This tree break, found by the author in the Jefferson National Forest, was about three inches in diameter and broken at a height of about six feet.

Speaking of Bigfoot juveniles, a Bedford County woman told the online outlet Cryptozoology News that she had recently spotted a "baby Bigfoot" and its mother. "The mom had to have seen me because I drove up on them," she said. "After she got away from the road headed toward the woods, she put the baby down, after about four steps." The witness was emphatic that what she saw was not a couple of bears: "There is no way this was a bear; I know bears and have seen them in the wild and this was no bear!" Whatever she saw had "light, brownish-red hair on the lower half hips down and dark hair up."

As you might expect, with its vast stretch of undisturbed wilderness areas, Shenandoah National Park has its share of Bigfoot sightings. In 2008, a woman reported to BFRO an encounter that she and her husband had in 1970 while driving on Skyline Drive. The following is an excerpt from report no. 24569:

> *We saw a large hairy thing. It looked like some of the pictures we have seen about bigfoot. We were so shocked we just stopped and then looked at each other and said what was that. We still remember this as if it happened yesterday. We know it was not a bear because it ran on two legs. It crossed the road in front of us and then ran down the side of the road and into the woods.*

The husband, called "Mr. J" in the report, described the creature as "six-feet tall, three hundred pounds, lanky, yet stocky, heavily muscled and with broad shoulders." The animal had deep brown hair, about two to three inches in length, and appeared muddy around its chest area.

The Phantoms and Monsters website has two reports from Shenandoah National Park. In the first, a man and his girlfriend had a harrowing encounter with a Bigfoot on a summer night in 2016—a traumatic experience after which the girlfriend has never been the same. The pair, camped in the Lewis Mountain Campground in Shenandoah National Park, was awakened after 1:00 a.m. to a crashing sound outside their tent. The man left the tent and shined his lantern and saw the camp stove was knocked over. Thinking nothing of it, he returned to the tent. Moments later, he heard a "chattering sound" that reminded him "of the sound a monkey makes when agitated." He got out of his tent again and saw a tall shadow walking on two legs. It made its way around the camp, making low grunting sounds. It then "materialized into a huge hairy beast" that lunged toward the couple.

The stunning view from Hawksbill Mountain, the highest point in Shenandoah National Park, with an elevation of 4,050 feet. Shenandoah National Park is noted for its Bigfoot sightings.

The pair retreated into the back of their tent, and the creature stayed around about another ten minutes before it left. They packed up and left at first light and haven't camped since. The witness contacted park authorities and recounted his story. Unsurprisingly, they dismissed it.

The other report took place in October 2017. A hiker in Shenandoah National Park was camped in a backcountry area in Rockingham County and was awakened after midnight by a sound that, he said, "scared the hell" out of him. He sat up in his tent and could hear rocks falling around him. He got out of his tent and heard heavy footsteps coming his way, so he rushed back and grabbed a .44 Magnum from his pack. He fired the gun in the opposite direction of the footsteps, and they stopped.

The hiker spent the night against a tree outside his tent with his weapon in his hand. At first light, he left without taking down his tent. On his way out, he heard the same noises that had awakened him and later saw an eight-foot hairy creature staring out at him. He took off running, and the monster belted out a horrible scream. "To this day I can still hear that scream," he said. "It sounded like a low growl at first, then continued into a high pitched shrill, becoming a long, sustained howling."

In August 2013, the online edition of the *Southwest Times* published a strange image of an unidentified animal that some think may have been a Bigfoot. A trail camera placed in a forested area in the mountains captured the picture, which shows a dark-colored animal bearing some resemblance to a gorilla. Editor Roger Williams asked, "What in the world can this be?" He went on to describe the image in an article titled "Unidentified Animal Seen on Trail Cam": "Carefully scrutinizing the image, it appears that the right arm shows fingers as the animal grasps the base of the tree stump. It also has elongated feet similar to a man's appendages. Its fur is matted on the back but thin on the arms and legs."

Unfortunately, the head and neck of the animal is not visible in the photograph, so it is not possible to identify the creature with 100 percent certainty. More likely than not, the animal was a bear; however, the publication of the image set off a rash of reports of sightings of a strange creature in the area.

One report came from Pulaski resident Steven Taylor. He was hunting in Wythe County when he saw something he had never seen before walk by his stand. It had matted fur with a bare chest and an oval-shaped head about the size of a basketball. The animal "strode on all fours until it reached a point near the top of the ridge." At that point, "it then stood up on its hind legs to better see the other side of the ridge and walked, upright, about ten or twelve yards before it returned to all fours and crossed the ridge top."

Taylor had been hesitant to share his experience with others; like countless witnesses who see something strange, he was afraid of ridicule.

Prompted by the picture that the *Southwest Times* published, Leroy Early wrote in and shared his encounter. Early heard a "guttural grunt" that attracted his attention and then saw something between six and seven feet in height standing on two legs. The furry creature was inspecting Early's chicken coop, perhaps thinking of grabbing an easy meal. Early's dog became frightened and took off running with its tail between its legs. Early retreated indoors and "made sure his shotgun was nearby." The creature ran off into the woods on two legs.

STORIES FROM WAY BACK

The term *Bigfoot* was coined in 1958 when the *Humboldt (CA) Times* used the word in an article about Jerry Crew, a tractor operator in California's remote Six Rivers National Forest who discovered tracks measuring sixteen inches in length. The term quickly caught on and became a household word. Stories of a bipedal apelike creature go much further back, however, to the earliest days of the nation, when pioneers saw strange hairy creatures in the forests. Native American tribes have tales of the creatures as well.

Newspapers in the 1800s and early 1900s ran many stories about "wild men." Most Bigfoot researchers believe that the old wild man stories are actually Bigfoot reports. In 1871, a Virginia paper, the *Petersburg Index*, ran a wild man story. The paper espoused a commonly held belief of the time that there was a "singular creature known as the 'Wild Man'" roaming the United States. The wild man was "superior to time and space, he thinks nothing of being seen simultaneously at points hundreds of miles apart." I suppose it did not occur to anyone that there might be multiple wild men and that these may not have been men at all—they were not human.

Wild man descriptions read very much like modern-day Bigfoot reports. According to the article, the wild man was "preternaturally hirsute"—in plain English, extremely hairy. He was also "ferocious, swift and strong" and had burning eyes; he "uttered unintelligible gibberish." As in Bigfoot reports today, the wild man was an expert at eluding capture and was skilled in the "game of hide and seek."

The wild man was known to stay "aloof from the settlements," content to keep his distance from people. Some speculated that he retreated to a home underground.

Something similar to the wild man, or Bigfoot, if you prefer, was on the loose in Washington County between 1868 and 1869. Some called it a "monster man," standing between seven and nine feet tall; it left twenty-inch footprints in the mud and had a pungent, distinct odor. Many believed this creature was a spirit or a ghost, due to the gray or white hair that covered its body.

The monster man set folks on edge when he began killing livestock. A man plowing a field helplessly watched as the creature snatched one of his goats and carried it off into the woods. The monster horrified an elderly lady when she saw it carry several chickens out of her chicken house. The encounter frightened her so badly that she moved in with one of her sons the following day.

In perhaps the most terrifying encounter, the monster man attacked a horse-drawn buggy. The couple inside managed to escape without harm, but the horse was not as fortunate. The monster tore it to shreds and ripped out a chunk of its neck and ate it.

The George Washington and Jefferson National Forests, managed as a single entity, are one of the largest areas of public land in the eastern United States. In Virginia, there are 1,664,110 acres of national forest land, providing an excellent habit for Bigfoot.

The creature drew the ire of the locals after breaking one of our longest held social taboos. A young man who had been ill since returning home from his service during the Civil War died and was buried on top of a mountain known for sightings of the monster. Within days, someone or something removed the body from the earth and stripped off its flesh! A heavily armed search party hunted the monster for days, to no avail, leading some to believe it lived in a cave with a hidden entrance.

The saga finally ended when a vicious storm blew through the area. No one saw the monster again after the storm—that is, until several years later, when hunters found an exceedingly large humanlike skeleton pinned beneath a fallen chestnut tree. It seems the monster met its end after getting caught in the storm.

One of the leading arguments that skeptics use to dispute the possibility that Bigfoot exists is to point out that no one has found a body. Perhaps a body has been found—by hunters in Washington County in the 1870s!

An interesting aspect of the Bigfoot that terrorized Washington County residents during the 1800s is its lightly colored coat. While most Bigfoot accounts tell of dark-colored or reddish-brown hair covering the creatures, there are some reports of white, gray and light tan coats, especially in southwestern Virginia, Kentucky and West Virginia. Is there a localized color variation among Bigfoot in this area? Is there a small population of albinos? There is no way to know the answer at this time; Bigfoot must first be proven to exist. But one thing is certain: the mountains of Virginia are a hotbed for sightings, and the reports cannot all be wrong. Something is out there.

3

WEREWOLVES AND DOGMEN

Angamanain is a very large Island. The people are without a king and are Idolaters, and no better than wild beasts. And I assure you all the men of this Island of Angamanain have heads like dogs, and teeth and eyes likewise; in fact, in the face they are all just like big mastiff dogs! They have a quantity of spices; but they are a most cruel generation, and eat everybody that they can catch, if not of their own race.
—*Marco Polo,* The Travels of Marco Polo

Throughout human history and in regions spanning the globe, tales of canine/human hybrids and humans able to shapeshift into canine, and part-canine form, have been a staple of our folklore. The tales stretch back deep into our past. Legendary figures such as Alexander the Great and Marco Polo supposedly encountered strange canine humanoids in the far-flung corners of the world.

Werewolf legends were prevalent in Europe during the Middle Ages and endured into the eighteenth century. Naturally, European folk beliefs—and their werewolf tales—came to America with the waves of immigrants who sought better lives and a fresh start on this far-off continent. This is evident in the Cajun legends of the rougarou, also called the loup-garou, a werewolf of sorts said to roam the swamps and cane fields of southern Louisiana. That said, Native American tribes have their own werewolf legends, such as the skin-walker of Navaho lore. The skin-walker is an evil witch that is able to shapeshift into animal form—often appearing as a wolf.

On the other end of the spectrum are dogmen—human/canine hybrids. These supposed creatures do not morph into a canine from human form,

An illustration of Alexander the Great doing battle with the dog-headed Cynophali in the late fifteenth century work *History of the Battles of Alexander the Great. Wikimedia Commons.*

but rather are some sort of hybrid species. In ancient and medieval times, there were supposed races of dog-headed men. In our day, stories of bipedal canines—sometimes standing over seven feet in height—stalking the forests of North America are spreading at a rapid pace.

Be it dogmen, werewolves or something between the two, the mountains of Virginia have their share of tales of these creatures—all the more reason to keep your eyes open and tread carefully when traversing secluded areas.

WEREWOLVES

Werewolves are much more common animals than you might think.
—Daniel Pinkwater

I was shocked after reading a headline in *USA Today* in the spring of 2019: "Murder Case Where Man Thought Victim Was a Werewolf Ends in

A engraving from the Mansell Collection, in London, of a werewolf devouring a woman. *Wikimedia Commons*.

Michael Wolgemut's illustration of a dog-headed man in Hartmann Schedel's 1493 book *The Nuremberg Chronicle. Wikimedia Commons.*

Mistrial." I had to do a double take and make sure I was reading a story from a credible news organization; this seemed more like a headline from the *Onion*. Alas, the story was true, and it was horrifying. Pankaj Bhasin, a thirty-four-year-old New Jersey resident, stabbed sixty-five-year-old Bradford Jackson, who managed a store in Alexandria, Virginia, fifty-three times and broke his neck. Bhasin claimed he saw Jackson turning into a werewolf, so he attacked him. He told police there was "still time to save ninety-nine percent of the moon and planets."

The jury in Bhasin's trial could not come to a consensus as to whether he was guilty of murder or not guilty of the charge by reason of insanity. The judge had no choice but to declare a mistrial.

Far from Old Town Alexandria, where the senseless tragedy occurred, in the westernmost reaches of the commonwealth, a werewolf story played out in the Cumberland Gap during the late 1800s—if the story can be believed. According to legend, something was stalking the forests, and locals blamed the creature for livestock deaths and the disappearance of several area women. A hunter caught a glimpse of the creature and believed it to be a mountain lion or possibly an escaped exotic animal from a traveling circus. Several months later, however, as he slept out under the stars, he was awakened to find the beast staring directly at him. He later claimed: "It was a wolf such as I had never seen. It was real, not a ghost."

The hunter grabbed his gun and managed to fire a shot as the wolf headed into the woods and vanished. Legend holds that when the hunter went looking for the wolf, he found no tracks but did happen upon some blood. Later analysis revealed the blood was from a human!

If this story can be believed, in light of the modern-day Bhasin murder trial, you have to wonder if the hunter, too, had attacked a man. It is a chilling thought.

The werewolf legend from the Cumberland Gap area pales in comparison to Virginia's most famous werewolf—the Henrico Werewolf. There is a long-standing tradition of a werewolf on the outskirts of Richmond in the Confederate Hills Recreation Area. Witnesses have spotted a six-foot-tall creature with a human-like body and a wolf head covered in dark, silver-tinged fur. Reports of the monster persist to this day.

Heading north from Richmond on U.S. 1 to the city of Woodbridge, a homeowner reported seeing some sort of animal in the woods in October 2011. He called the police. According to news reports:

> *Officers were called late Monday to the area of Colchester Road and Randall Drive in Woodbridge after a neighbor reported seeing something suspicious.*
>
> *"A coyote, or a werewolf," said Prince William County police spokesman Jonathan Perok. "The resident said they spotted the creature in the woods at 10:05 p.m."*
>
> *Authorities came out and checked out the area and saw no signs of a possible coyote.*

Police saw no signs of a coyote. That is to be expected in a densely populated city in northern Virginia. But did they look for evidence of a werewolf prowling the woods? Probably not. Maybe they should have.

WHAT? WERE YOU RAISED BY WOLVES?

Maybe even weirder than the werewolf tales are stories of wolf children. Of course, stories of wild children go way back and have made their way into popular culture through films such as *Nell*, a 1994 movie set in the Smoky Mountains starring Jodie Foster and Liam Neeson. However, a story from eighteenth-century Virginia tops the movie. In the tale, two young girls whose parents had died were found living in the wild in a swampy area. The girls survived by eating roots and fish and communicated with one another using a system of sounds and signs. After being taken in and brought to civilization, the girls "were become domestic" and taught to speak English.

In a similar, yet stranger tale, around the turn of the twentieth century, hunters in the mountains of Virginia came upon a wolf nursing two young girls about two years of age. The wolf ran away as the hunters approached, and the girls tensed up and growled at the men. A man in the hunting party agreed to take the girls home and look after them. Sadly, one of the girls died of pneumonia only a few months later.

Years went by, and the surviving girl, named Annette, was engaged to be married. But as fate would have it, the call of the wild seduced Annette, who returned to her feral ways. She and her fiancé were walking through the woods when the couple encountered a pack of wolves. Several wolves let out a howl. Rather than being frightened, Annette ran to them. She was never seen again.

DOGMEN

Dogmen can be distinguished from werewolves in that they are "full-time" beings, not shapeshifters. A couple of decades ago, reports of dogmen seemed sporadic and were mostly confined to Wisconsin and Michigan. Today, however, dogmen are spotted almost anywhere and with frequency rivaling Bigfoot sightings. Perhaps the internet has played a role in spreading the dogman legend; undoubtedly, it has helped bring more encounters to light with the growing number of reporting sites and websites that help spread general awareness.

There have been a host of dogman sightings in the mountains of Virginia. Reports go back further than most would imagine. Residents of Lynchburg were on edge in the spring of 1885 when several witnesses claimed to have seen "a monster—half man and half dog—running about the city at night trying to eat small boys."

The Virginia Chapter of the North American Dogman Project has several reports on its website. In the early 1980s, a man driving through southwestern Virginia was chased by a dogman. He claimed the creature "could keep pace with his muscle car." Also in southwestern Virginia, multiple witnesses claimed they saw a dogman jump across cars on a country road in 2017. The following report from Danville is especially frightening:

> *1990 in Danville, Virginia, a woman called the police to report "something" had dragged her dog off. When the on duty police officer arrived he went into the wood line to look for the woman's dog. He heard a crunching noise and saw a dogman. He had a shotgun with him and shot at the creature. A pellet must have hit his eye because the dogman was blinking. The creature let off a loud howl/growl and ran away on all fours.*

Three Madison County women claimed to see a dogman while exploring an old abandoned mill. The trio saw a "big gray furry creature that looked like it was hunched over" in one of the rooms. Dogman eyewitnesses often state the creatures possess glowing eyes, some red in color, others amber or yellow. The same holds true in the Madison County report; the creature had glowing yellow eyes. Further descriptions of the beast indicated it had "big meaty shoulders" and "humanoid hands," and one witness noticed a tail.

The women fled the scene on seeing the dogman and returned home. The woman who came forward with the story said that, later that night:

> *My sister drew a sketch of what she saw, and was doing some tarot readings after we got home. She had her cards stacked on her sketchbook and a bug crawled on it and started going crazy running around until it stepped on the top card on the deck, then it stopped moving. My friend picked up the top card and it was the wolfman card of my sister's Native American tarot deck.*

There are many who think the appearance of dogmen or other creatures whose origins seem to be supernatural can be brought on by occult practices such as reading tarot cards. There is probably no way to know if this is true or if the dogman encounter in this case was related in any way to tarot readings.

A dogman, thought by some to be the infamous "Kentucky Wolfman," has been spotted near the Kentucky line on the outskirts of Pound, Virginia. In one encounter, the dogman tried to attack a motorist. While driving to his grandfather's house at around 3:00 a.m., a man claimed to see a furry creature along the road. It had glowing golden-greenish eyes, long claws, doglike feet and legs, a long snout and long, sharp teeth covered in blood.

At first, the witness thought he had fallen asleep and was dreaming, and though he was about to live through a nightmare, what transpired was real and "one hundred percent completely true."

The creature smirked and then leapt onto the hood of the witness' car. It swatted at the windshield and door, so the driver shifted into reverse and floored the accelerator. He then slammed the brake pedal and threw the monster off the car and drove as fast as he could down Rat Creek Road. Incredibly, the dogman followed him and caught up to the vehicle. It grabbed the bumper, so the driver hit the brakes and sent the monster tumbling over the front of the car. As the man sped away, the dogman jumped onto a high tree limb and then dove on top of the car once again.

From here, the story really gets weird. The dogman spoke in a raspy voice and yelled at the driver, demanding he stop the car. Once again, the driver slammed on the brakes and flung the dogman from the vehicle. This time, he ran over the creature's legs and sped away, heading toward Pound. The dogman pursued the motorist for a while but eventually gave up the chase and let out a howl.

Whatever one thinks of this story, the other encounters in this chapter or the dogman phenomenon as a whole, sightings of the creatures are far more common than most realize. A couple of years ago, an investigator told me of a rash of sightings in western Pennsylvania, one of which was quite chilling. A bowhunter was up in his tree stand and looked down to see an upright canine walking through the woods. It had piercing yellow eyes and was an incredible ten feet tall. It stopped and locked eyes with the hunter before finally leaving and going about its way.

There are many in the cryptozoology community who attribute dogman sightings to misidentified Bigfoot sightings, while others dismiss the encounters altogether. In November 2018, I attended AlienCon in Baltimore, Maryland, and visited the Sasquatch Syndicate booth. Dr. Jeffrey Meldrum, professor of anatomy and anthropology at Idaho State University, was manning the booth. I spoke with him about dogman reports and asked his opinion on the matter. He picked up a large cast of a Bigfoot track and said: "Well, with these supposed dogman sightings, you just don't get tracks. I ask people,

The author discussing dogman sightings with Dr. Jeffrey Meldrum at AlienCon in Baltimore, Maryland, in November 2018.

where are the tracks? The tracks don't lie." In my conversation with him, he seemed to attribute most of today's dogman stories to werewolf lore and cultural legends such as the rougarou and skin-walkers.

Myself, I tend to think that if dogmen exist, they are paranormal in nature rather than flesh-and-blood animals lurking in the forest. But whatever they are and wherever they come from, one thing is certain—they are not going away anytime soon, and the reports are spreading. Why?

4

PHANTOM DOGS

One striking aspect of the stories is how similar their descriptions of ghostly dogs are. The dogs are always large and black, and they have remarkable eyes, which are variously described as being red, "as big as saucers," and "shining like balls of fire."
—Thomas E. Barden, Virginia Folk Legends

There is a long-standing tradition of ghostly black dogs in Europe, and they appear quite often in stories from the British Isles. Phantom black dogs such as the Black Shuck and Barguest are prominent in British folklore. These dogs are described as having luminous eyes and large fangs. The beasts are enormous, said to be the size of a calf, and shriek and howl at night, sometimes accompanied by the sound of chains. In some cases, the phantom dog appears after the death of a notable person.

In 1578, Abraham Fleming, a London clergyman, published a chilling tale in a pamphlet titled *A Strange and Terrible Wunder*. It was the retelling of a bizarre incident that occurred in the Parish Church of St. Mary in Bungay:

> *there appeered in a most horrible similitude and likenesse to the congregation then and there present a dog as they might discerne it, of a black colour:… This black dog or the divil in such a likenesses…passed between two persons as they were kneeling upon their knees, and occupied in prayer as it seemed wrung the necks of them bothe at one instant clene backward in so much that even at a moment where they kneeled they strangley died.*

Sightings of black phantom dogs are still reported in Great Britain to this day. George Eberhart chronicled several of these encounters in his work *Mysterious Creatures: A Guide to Cryptozoology*, including the following account from 1991: "Victoria Rice-Heaps encountered a huge Black dog with glowing red eyes as she was driving past Hodsock Priory near Worksop, Nottinghamshire, England, early in the morning of May 11, 1991. It was about 18 inches taller than a great dane and seemed to be dragging something across the road."

America, too, has its share of phantom black dogs. Most believe that European immigrants brought their tales of canine apparitions to the New World. Oftentimes, these beasts are malevolent, or at least seem to be, but in the mountains of Virginia, there are a couple of tales that depart from the norm and are heartwarming.

LOYAL TO THE END AND THEN SOME!

A young man from the Shenandoah Valley returned home following his service in the European theater of the Second World War. Not knowing he had returned—the young man wanted to surprise his folks—no one from his family was at the train station to give him a ride home. So, he set out walking on a dark, moonless night. As he walked along the river road near his home, he could hear the gushing currents and could tell the river was swollen from the spring rains.

The young man came to a new bridge, which would be a considerable shortcut, and there he was met by his old dog, Shep. Shep lunged with excitement and tackled the young man. After the reunion with his furry friend, he gathered himself and began to walk toward the bridge, but Shep blocked the way and began barking incessantly and tugged at his pants leg. Shep refused to budge, and finally, the young man decided to take the long way home and cross the old bridge farther down the road. Shep happily walked the young man to the front door and then went about his way.

It was a wonderful reunion, and after catching up with everyone, the young man explained that he would have been home sooner, but Shep made him take the long way home. The entire room stared at him, and his mother turned pale. "Old Shep is dead, son. He died last winter," his father explained.

The following morning, the young man and his father walked out to the new bridge. The pair immediately saw a large, gaping hole in the center of the span. Had the young man taken this route, he would have stepped right through the hole and been swept away in the ferocious currents. He would have died without anyone knowing he had even made it home from the war. Ever the good boy, Shep came back from the grave to ensure that his old buddy made it home safe.

My favorite phantom dog tale is that called "Black Dog of the Blue Ridge." It is a heartbreaking yet heartwarming tale of another loyal companion—a true friend to the end. Mrs. R.F. Herrick recounted the tale in the *Journal of American Folklore* in 1907:

> *In Botetourt County, Virginia, there is a pass that was much traveled by people going to Bedford County and by visitors to mineral springs in the vicinity. In the year 1683, the report was spread that at the wildest part of the trail in this pass there appeared at sunset a great black dog, who, with majestic tread, walked in a listening attitude about two hundred feet and then turned and walked back. Thus he passed back and forth like a sentinel on guard, always appearing at sunset to keep his nightly vigil and disappearing again at dawn. And so the whispering went with bated breath from one to another, until it had traveled from one end of the state to the other.*
>
> *Parties of young cavaliers were made up to watch for the black dog. Many saw him. Some believed him to be a veritable dog sent by some master to watch; others believed him to be a witch dog. A party decided to go through the pass at night, well-armed, to see if the dog would molest them. Choosing a night when the moon was full, they mounted good horses and sallied forth. Each saw a great dog larger than any they had ever seen. Clapping spurs to their horses, they rode forward. But they had not calculated on the fear of their steeds. When they approached the dog, the horses snorted with fear, and, in spite of whip, spur, and rein, gave him a wide berth as he marched on as serenely as if no one was near. The party was unable to force their horses to take the pass again until after daylight. Then they were laughed at by their comrades to whom they told their experiences. They decided to lie in ambush, kill the dog and bring in his hide.*
>
> *The next night found the young men well hidden behind rocks and bushes with guns in hand. As the last ray of sunlight kissed the highest peak of the Blue Ridge, the black dog appeared at the lower end of his walk and came majestically toward them. When he came opposite, every gun cracked. When the smoke cleared away, the great dog was turning at the end of his walk, seemingly unconscious of the presence of the hunters. Again and*

again they fired, and still, the dog walked his beat, and fear caught the hearts of the hunters, and they fled wildly away to their companions, and the black dog held the pass at night unmolested.

Time passed, and year after year went by, until seven years had come and gone, when a beautiful woman came over from the old country, trying to find her husband who eight years before had come to make a home for her in the new land. She traced him to Bedford County, and from there all trace of him was lost. Many remembered the tall, handsome man and his dog. Then there came to her ear the tale of the vigil of the great dog of the mountain pass, and she pleaded with the people to take her to see him, saying that if he was her husband's dog, he would know her.

A party was made up, and before night they arrived at the gap. The lady dismounted and walked to the place where the nightly watch was kept. As the shadows grew long, the party fell back on the trail, leaving the lady alone, and as the sun sank into his purple bed of splendor the great dog appeared. Walking to the lady, he laid his great head in her lap for a moment, then turning he walked a short way from the trail, looking back to see that she was following. He led her until he paused by a large rock, where he gently scratched the ground, gave a long, low wail, and disappeared. The lady called the party to her and asked them to dig. As they had no implements, and she refused to leave, one of them rode back for help. When they dug below the surface, they found the skeleton of a man and the hair and bones of a great dog. They found a seal ring on the hand of the man and a heraldic embroidery in silk that the wife recognized. She removed the bones for proper burial and returned to her old home. It was never known who had killed the man. But from that time to this the great dog, having finished his faithful work has never appeared again.

If only we could all have a friend like Shep or the Black Dog of the Blue Ridge. As they say, "we don't deserve dogs."

THE SNARLY YOW

A dark—and more common—manifestation of the phantom dog phenomenon is the Snarly Yow, a ghostly dog whose origins can be traced to Wales. The creature is an enormous dog, black in color, with a "fierce red mouth," large paws and glowing eyes. The Snarly Yow is much more

Beware of the "Snarly Yow"
Legend has it that the shadow of a black dog used to prowl the heights of South Mountain. One night, a huntsman, famous as a sure shot, encountered the beast. He aimed and fired his rifle. The shot went right through the animal with no effect. He fired again and again, each shot passing through the shadowy beast. Finally, overcome with dread, the huntsman fled.

This sidebar appears on a Civil War historical marker alongside U.S. 40 in Boonsboro, Maryland.

a Maryland legend than one of Virginia, as the creature haunts the South Mountain area. However, the Snarly Yow warrants mention in this book, as it has been spotted as far south as Hillsboro, Virginia, especially in the early twentieth century. Moreover, witnesses to this day occasionally see the Snarly Yow in the vicinity of Harpers Ferry, West Virginia, where Maryland, Virginia and West Virginia meet.

The Snarly Yow legend took off in the tristate area in the early 1900s, when folks began seeing a massive black dog with a red mouth. It would often leap in front of travelers, only to disappear into the darkness of the night. The phantom dog never harmed anyone, although it did frighten everyone who crossed its path. Many tried hitting the beast with sticks and stones; some even attempted to shoot it. However, projectiles passed right through the canine apparition. In Boonsboro, Maryland, the sidebar of a roadside Civil War historical marker tells of a huntsman who tried to shoot the Snarly Yow:

> *Beware of the "Snarly Yow"*
> *Legend has it that the shadow of a black dog used to prowl the heights of South Mountain. One night, a huntsman, famous as a sure shot, encountered the beast. He aimed and fired his rifle. The shot went right through the animal with no effect. He fired again and again, each shot passing through the shadowy beast. Finally overcome with dread, the huntsman fled.*

In recent times, motorists driving along U.S. 40 and U.S. 15 have had encounters in which the Snarly Yow suddenly appeared in front of their vehicles. In at least one instance, the vehicle seemingly hit the creature, but when the driver turned around to look, the phantom dog was standing in the lane as if the car had passed right through its body.

5

OTHER STRANGE CREATURES

Gorillas were once considered mythical creatures.
—National Cryptid Society

There are many cryptids, out-of-place animals and entities that seem paranormal in nature that do not fit into convenient categories such as big cats, dogmen and Bigfoot. Think about it: in what category do you place something that witnesses describe as part Bigfoot and part goat? Then there are creatures that could be easily categorized but sightings of which are not as widespread as big cats and Bigfoot. Naturally, a few of these beasts and entities are lurking in the dark hollows and thickly wooded hillsides deep in Virginia's mountains. To close out this part of the book, I will discuss several of these enigmatic creatures in the paragraphs to follow.

DEVIL MONKEYS

My friend was so obviously shaken that I had no choice but to believe him.
—James Boyd

Let's assume that Bigfoot is real and roaming the heavily forested Virginia mountains, and that the creature is a yet-to-be-discovered species of great ape. Do you wonder, then, if a great ape is loose in the woods, could there also be smaller primates, maybe even swinging through the trees? If the reports are true, this is exactly the case, and these creatures have a name: devil monkeys.

Devil monkey descriptions vary quite a bit among witnesses. Some describe a baboon-like creature, while others claim what they saw looked like a lemur. There are even reports that the creature looked like a wild dog from a distance. Sometimes, witnesses report seeing a long tail on the animal; others make no mention of tails. Size estimates of devil monkeys vary, as well; figures range from three feet in length all the way up to eight feet. While there is a great deal of inconsistency among the witness descriptions of devil monkeys, a number of physical characteristics are commonly reported: dark hair, with white hair on the neck and belly; a doglike snout; pointed ears; and long teeth and claws. Another common trait observed among devil monkeys is aggression, hence the "devil" moniker. These creatures can be vicious and are known to attack people, pets and livestock without provocation. Some believe that devil monkeys were the culprit behind a rash of killings of dogs, cats and livestock that occurred in the 1930s in Virginia, Tennessee and Kentucky.

Devil monkeys are spotted nationwide, but the Appalachian Mountains seem to be a hot spot. From as far back as the 1920s, these enigmatic creatures have been seen in Tennessee, Kentucky, Ohio, West Virginia, New Hampshire and other states. Perhaps the most chilling devil monkey reports come from Smyth County, Virginia. Here, a devil monkey attacked motorists in 1959.

The first incident began when Paulette Boyd's parents were driving on a bright moonlit night and something sprang toward their car window. The creature pressed its face against the passenger window, grasped the side of the car with its claws and, amazingly, kept speed with the vehicle for a period of time. The animal's hair was taffy-colored with a white underbelly. It had muscular legs, and its front legs were shorter than its back legs. When the encounter ended and the Boyds examined their car, three long scratches—down to the base metal—ran the entire length of the car.

The Boyds may have been the first to have a run-in with the devil monkey, but they would not be the last. Several days after their encounter, two nurses in Saltville were attacked by the crazed monkey as they drove home from work. The pair was riding in a convertible, and the monkey jumped onto their car and ripped off the top. Thankfully, no one suffered an injury in the attack.

The locals were greatly concerned about the attacks and formed a search party to locate the creature. Their attempts to find the monkey menace failed. Oddly, the dogs brought to track the devil monkey refused to follow its trail.

Fourteen years later, a devil monkey surfaced along a mountain road between Tazewell and Marion. In this incident, the driver had his window down and arm hanging out, heading up the mountain from Marion. About halfway up the mountain, a noise outside the car caught his attention, and that is when he saw an animal matching the descriptions from the earlier Saltville attacks. The monkey ran from the edge of the woods to his car and took a swipe at his arm. The driver recounted, "I was so scared I mashed the accelerator to the floor and never let up till I reached the town of Richlands."

Most believe that devil monkeys are exotic pets that escaped or possibly escapees from zoos or circuses. However, in and around Smyth County, sporadic devil monkey sightings continued to occur into the late 1990s, indicating that there might be a small breeding population in the mountains. A chilling thought.

An Ohio woman saw a devil monkey while driving through Roanoke late at night in 1994. The sighting took place along a two-lane country road, after she had been redirected by a construction detour. The witness claimed a black creature resembling a wolf-monkey hybrid jumped in front of her car. It had short, sleek fur with a long tail and pointy ears. The animal was very large; according to the witness, standing on its hind legs, it easily reached six feet in height. Allegedly, shortly after the encounter, area livestock began to go missing.

Several hours to the east, in Goochland County, residents began seeing devil monkeys in 2010. The Goochland County Devil Monkey Official Sightings Blog logged nearly ten sightings in early December. The Goochland Public Safety Network responded to a post on the blog, saying:

> *New information is emerging about the unidentified animal prowling Goochland County. Sighting frequency has increased, with the latest accounts showing movement westward from the Gum Spring area to Hadensville along the Rt. 250 corridor.*
>
> *GPSN has increased the threat level to Orange. Keep small children and pets inside and away from doors and windows. Those in outlying areas should exercise extreme caution at all times. Only go outdoors when alert and fully armed.*
>
> *Please report additional sightings to GPSN. Include time, date, location, and description.*

Could a white-nosed coati be responsible for the devil monkey sightings in Goochland County? *Photograph by Benjamin Keen, Wikimedia Commons.*

Another round of devil monkey sightings took place in Goochland County in 2014. This time, however, the creature in question may have been identified. Donovan Paul Yates wrote a letter to the editor of the *Richmond Times-Dispatch*, believing he had solved the riddle. Yates claimed to have spotted the creature during the 2010 flap. "I have seen this species of animal before. It is a South American Coatimundi."

Coatimundi? Lemur? Baboon? Wolf-monkey hybrid? What are we dealing with in southwestern Virginia and to the east in Goochland County? Are these exotic out-of-place animals from zoos or private collections, or are they something more sinister—perhaps a genetic experiment gone awry? Unfortunately, there are more questions than answers, and it seems that, for now, at least, this is how it will remain.

So, if you are in the woods and hear monkey noises, do not doubt what you have heard—you aren't going crazy. Trust your senses and then get the hell out of there!

SHEEPSQUATCH

Sheepsquatch. You do not have to be a grizzled cryptozoologist or a lifelong paranormal investigator to figure out what this unique creature is. If you guessed a bipedal cross between a sheep and a Sasquatch, then you are correct!

Sheepsquatch came to prominence in the early to mid-1990s after a rash of sightings in the West Virginia counties of Mason, Boone, Kanawha and Putnam. Eyewitnesses described a creature the size of a bear with wooly, white fur and horns like a ram or goat. The weird beast has been spotted both walking upright and on all fours, and some who have seen it claim that it has pawlike hands.

In one of the earliest and most cited reports, Ed Rollins, from Gallipolis, Ohio, saw a strange creature at a former munitions facility on the outskirts of Point Pleasant, West Virginia. If Point Pleasant sounds familiar, it is because it was the scene of a catastrophic 1967 bridge collapse that killed forty-six people. The infamous creature dubbed "Mothman" had been spotted around Point Pleasant for thirteen months leading up to the disaster. Rollins originally went to the grounds of the old munitions plant, known locally as the TNT area, to investigate Mothman. What he found was much different.

As Rollins walked through a brushy area along a creek, he saw a four-legged creature with brownish-white, matted fur emerge from the woods. It had pawlike hands and a pointed face with horns atop its head. Rollins observed the animal take a drink of water, and as soon as it finished and was on its way, he ran to his vehicle.

Maybe the strangest aspect of Rollins's encounter was that he claimed Sheepsquatch smelled of sulfur. Perhaps it was something in the water or the residual effects of the manufacture of munitions from previous years. However, the smell of sulfur is a hallmark of demonology and occult literature, and the smell often accompanies demonic activity, ghosts and other paranormal entities, and is even present after some UFO and alien encounters.

In 2015, several campers in Fulks Run, Virginia, a small community in Rockingham County bounded by the George Washington National Forest, had a Sheepsquatch encounter. One of the campers saw a weird animal crouched on a hillside around midnight. He went to warn the others in the group, and as he did, the creature stood up and ran down the hill toward their camp. When standing, the creature was eight to nine feet tall. According to the report, a river (presumably the North Fork of the Shenandoah River) lay between Sheepsquatch and the camp, halting the creature's progress.

The campers gathered together and watched Sheepsquatch as it waded across the river. When it emerged from the water, the witnesses said it looked like a white dog with long fur standing on two legs. The encounter ended when a loud, eerie shriek rang out in the woods, sending Sheepsquatch scurrying back into the forest.

In 2014, a Sheepsquatch sighting occurred in Fairy Stone State Park in Patrick County. Teena and a friend were hiking on a secluded trail in the park when they noticed something move about fifty yards in front of them. It was large and bulky and lightly colored. Moments later, the pair got a good look at the creature when it moved onto a rock. It was as large as a medium-sized bear with yellowish-gray fur. The animal had a long snout and dark, round eyes set lower on its head than a bear.

With this, Teena and her friend fled the park and headed directly home. Teena said of the encounter: "The creature is unlike any I have seen or heard about before. I had made an inquiry to a local historian who laughed and said I saw a 'Sheep Squatch.' What is that?"

What is that? Indeed. There are no easy answers to the Sheepsquatch enigma. It would seem the creature is a paranormal entity of some kind rather than a flesh-and-blood animal. Another thought is that it might be a Bigfoot—if Bigfoot exists and is an undiscovered animal itself. Recall from earlier the accounts of sightings of lightly colored Bigfoots in southwestern Virginia, particularly the strange tale from Washington County in the late 1800s. Is this an adequate answer for Sheepsquatch sightings? Unfortunately, there is simply no way to know at this time.

WINGED HUMANOIDS, THUNDERBIRDS AND PTEROSAURS

Winged creatures are a staple of the world of the unexplained. Winged humanoids make their appearance in the skies, the most famous being the Mothman. Mothman made its rounds over the skies of Point Pleasant, West Virginia, and the surrounding area in the late 1960s. The flap occurred around the time the Silver Bridge collapsed and fell into the icy waters of the Ohio River, killing forty-six people, on December 15, 1967.

Since that time, Mothman has made appearances all over, and a similar creature has been spotted around Lake Michigan in recent years. Mothman has largely avoided the commonwealth of Virginia, although there was a rash of possible sightings in a wooded area of southwestern Fairfax County in the late 1990s and early 2000s.

Other common mysterious winged creatures are massive birds—too large to be anything known to currently fly through the skies of Virginia. Often called "thunderbirds," the enormous birds have wingspans topping twenty feet and are covered in dark feathers. Some believe these are surviving teratorns, large birds of prey that supposedly died out at the end of the last ice age.

There are tales of small children being carried away by large birds, and without a doubt, this has fed into thunderbird lore. A story from Wise County comes to mind. Works Progress Administration writer James Taylor Adams recounted a tale from Royce Cress that he received on February 2, 1942:

> *Mother told me that one time there was a man an' a woman an' they had a little baby. The man an' woman had to go out in the meadow and cut hay an' rake it up, an' they laid the baby in the shade. They kept noticing a big eagle sailin' around and around. Hit come down lower an' lower. They never thought of anything. Then all at once the eagle come down with a swoop an' carried the baby off. The woman started screamin' an' the man startin' hollerin', an' they both started runnin'. They seen the old eagle flyin' way back in the mountain to where there was a big high cliff. The man an' woman run to the foot of the mountain and they clomb an' clomb an' clomb. At last they got to the cliff an' the man told the woman to wait there, an' he climb hand over hand up the side of the cliff. They seen the old eagle fly off again, an' when the man got to the nest, there laid the baby in the nest with the young eagles. They hadn't bothered hit, an' the man just got it an' clomb back down the cliff with it.*

Another aspect of the mysterious winged creature phenomenon are pterosaurs gliding through the skies. As unbelievable as it may sound for these flying lizards to be alive millions of years after their supposed extinction, they are spotted with a staggering frequency—some reports have occurred in Virginia. A Virginia woman claimed to see something unforgettable late one night while swimming in a reservoir when she was seventeen years old. A large silhouette appeared in the sky with wings that stretched fifteen to twenty feet. With just a few flaps, it covered a great distance. The creature had batlike wings, was free of feathers and had a pointed head and long, sharp talons. The witness said, "I have not before nor since ever been so petrified in my life."

A Virginia man claimed to see two of these creatures flying in the air in 2012. He said, "The most obvious feature was the diamond or spade tipped tail, I have not found any creature that compares."

A wave of supposed pterosaur sightings occurred recently in western North Carolina, with a few in the Asheville area. Perhaps the tales from the early 1900s of "snallygasters"—flying creatures that were supposedly half-bird and half-reptile—are related to these modern-day pterosaur reports. As bizarre as it all sounds, you have to wonder what is going on in the skies.

BELLED BUZZARDS

It is not something that is reported anymore—not widely, at least—but tales of "belled buzzards" were prevalent in the Appalachian Mountains in the late 1800s and early 1900s. These strange and frightful creatures were turkey vultures with bells around their necks and often perceived as harbingers of death. The *Lexington Gazette* reported on March 18, 1903: "A belled buzzard was seen in several sections of Rockbridge County last year. Mr. James Hill, who lives near Ruffner schoolhouse, says it made its appearance last Friday near his home. This buzzard has a peculiar affinity for Lexington magisterial district, as it was seen several weeks ago about East Lexington."

On March 16, 1894, the *Shenandoah Herald* asked, "Who belled the buzzard?" The paper gave the following account: "Mr. George Afflick, while working on his farm last week, heard the sound of a small bell above him, in the air. On looking up, he saw five or six buzzards, one of which had a bell on. We are anxious to know who belled him."

On October 27, 1887, the *Alexandria Gazette* reported that a belled buzzard was spotted in the company of about fifty other buzzards at a farm in western Fauquier County. Earlier in the year, on March 2, the same paper ran a piece in which someone shot and killed a belled buzzard in Texas. The article described the bell in detail and provided clues as to where the buzzard came from.

> *The bell was well toned, of brass, and about two and a half inches across the base. It was hung to the bird by a copper wire, twisted around its neck. There was no chafing, the skin being protected by an abundance of down; "1879" was scratched on the narrow, flat top of the bell. The last heard of the bird was in Virginia, a short time ago, and it was presumably on its way south at that time.*

A belled buzzard was spotted in Fishersville in 1902. E. Fielding and several friends saw the bird with about twelve others flying south, and the sound of a bell was "distinct and clear." In 1905, onlookers saw a belled buzzard in the vicinity of Winchester. Some believed it to be the same buzzard that had been caught and belled in Albemarle County sometime earlier. The *Shenandoah Herald* reported on March 5, 1905:

> *I have frequently noticed accounts of a belled buzzard I think that must be the same buzzard that was caught and belled by Mr. Agnes Sprouse on her*

farm about two miles from White Hall, Albemarle County. I have seen it several times fly over my mill in the mountains near Mr. Sprouse's home. This buzzard I refer to was caught and belled about five years ago, a small sheep bell being put on with a strap and wire.

The Winchester area experienced a large number of belled buzzard sightings in 1922, as did nearby Hardy County, West Virginia. Several sightings also occurred in Jefferson County, West Virginia, near the towns of Charles Town and Harpers Ferry.

Sightings of belled buzzards continued well into the 1930s and even into the early 1940s, though the frequency of the reports had waned. In 1931, newspapers across the nation reported the death of a belled buzzard hit by an automobile in Indiana:

Traditional stories of a mysterious "belled buzzard," a bird allied to the vulture, which in some manner acquired a small bell firmly to its neck, appeared to be verified when an automobile owned by Rufus Turner, of Spencer, Ind., struck and killed such a bird near that city. A small bell, indicated by the arrow in the above picture, was buckled to the buzzard's neck by a strap. How the bell got there, Turner makes no pretense of knowing. However, the mysterious tinkling sound from the sky that has been reported from time to time for years in many states, may have been real.

The belled buzzard phenomenon is easily explainable, as there are many reports of folks capturing a buzzard and affixing a bell to its neck. How you would go about catching a buzzard is beyond me. Moreover, it seems strange that anyone would want to do such a thing in the first place, but once the trend got started, tricksters must have been eager to carry on the tradition. For an unsuspecting person to hear a bell ringing, and then to see a large buzzard flying overhead—perhaps circling in its slow and eerie way—must have been a troubling encounter, to say the least.

"ONE-OFFS"

The mountains of Virginia hold a variety of what I call "one-offs"—creatures for which a tale or two exists, but nothing that comes close to a rash of sightings, and the few accounts are confined to a specific geographic location. A few one-offs that come to mind are a reptilian humanoid spotted by a girl in Luray in 2002; a creature described as a gargoyle in Bluefield; a chupacabra—the "goat sucker" of Latin American folklore—that was spotted recently in Bridgewater; and a witness saw something the size of a bear, "kind of like Bigfoot," white in color with glowing red eyes in a Berryville park a couple of years ago. Maybe the most bizarre of all are the tales of a troll lurking in Lynchburg. And by troll, I am referring to the trolls of fairy lore, not an annoying person who leaves inflammatory comments on social media sites. There are more one-offs than I can recount, and new ones come along all the time—a report of a two-tailed, large rodent-like creature even came across my desk.

It is clear to see that the mountains of Virginia have their share of cryptids, out-of-place animals and flat-out bizarre entities roaming around. New ones come along quite often, and the old and forgotten can reappear at any moment. Who knows? Maybe you will be next to witness something strange.

Part II

HIDDEN HISTORY

6

GIANTS, MOUNDS AND MORE

It seems a great pity now that our ancestors preserved so few of the Indian names. "Tuscarora Creek," "Shawnee Spring," "Massanutten Mountain," and "Shenandoah Valley" are certainly beautiful enough to make us wish for others from the same musical languages; but these are nearly all that have been preserved in this immediate region.
—*John W. Wayland,* A History of Shenandoah County, Virginia

Ancient America was far different than most of us have been taught to believe. We tend to think of the Americas as having small villages separated by great distances and vast wilderness areas before the age of European colonization. In reality, the opposite is true. When Columbus landed on the shores of the New World in 1492, there may have been more than 110 million people living in the Americas. Even using conservative estimates, scholars place the number of inhabitants at around 60 million. Moreover, the Americas had many cities, even city-states, and some of these had populations that rival our cities today. At its peak between the years CE 1200 and 1500, the renowned city of the Mississippian culture, Cahokia, located in modern-day Illinois, exceeded the size of London and had a population of 20,000. Some think the number of residents was closer to 50,000.

When the Spanish began their explorations into the southeastern United States in the 1500s, they wrote of many well-populated towns close to one another. When the next generation of explorers visited the same areas, most of these towns were abandoned, and the native populations had significantly declined. Diseases, especially smallpox, decimated staggering numbers of people. In later years, westward expansion, and finally Manifest Destiny, took its toll on the indigenous people. Sadly, much ancient history and sacred knowledge was forever lost to future generations. What we can be sure of, however, is that ancient America was quite advanced, and its history is complex. Hundreds, even thousands of years before Columbus, there were visitors to the Americas, some of whom established trade with various tribes. There were great cities and high cultures in place; mounds, geometrically designed earthworks and even pyramids stood tall against the landscape; terrible wars occurred; and there were giants in the land.

THERE WERE GIANTS IN THOSE DAYS

The eyes of that species of extinct giants, whose bones fill the mounds of America, have gazed on Niagara, as ours do now. Contemporary with the whole race of men, and older than the first man, Niagara is strong, and fresh today as ten thousand years ago.
—Abraham Lincoln

According the Bible, in the sixth chapter of Genesis, "there were giants in the earth in those days." When folks think of this often-cited passage, it is usually the David and Goliath story that comes to mind. Or, on a lighter note, people think of the giant in the "Jack and the Beanstalk" tale. While giant Philistines and giants living in castles in the clouds may be the first thought on the subject, ancient America had its share of tales of giants roaming the land, and undoubtedly, some of them walked the ridgelines of Virginia's mountains. While Virginia's neighbors Kentucky and, especially, West Virginia, are better known for their giant discoveries, the Old Dominion can boast a few as well.

According to Hu Maxwell and H.L. Swisher's *History of Hampshire County, West Virginia*, which recounts many exceedingly large skeletal finds in the area, a human thighbone measuring thirty-six inches was unearthed along Flint Run in present-day Warren County, Virginia. A thighbone that size could only have come from a guy or gal who stood around nine and a half feet tall.

To the north, in Winchester, soldiers discovered the remains of giants in the 1750s. During the French and Indian War, Indian groups aligned with the French attacked settlements on the frontier, and the town of Winchester

This historical marker in downtown Winchester pays tribute to Fort Loudoun, designed by a young Colonel George Washington.

was selected as the site of a fort to protect the local citizenry. The fort was strong and heavily armed with twenty-four cannons. Colonel George Washington, the commander of the Virginia regiment, designed the fort and supervised its construction. The regiment named it Fort Loudoun in honor of Governor General of Virginia and Commander in Chief John Campbell, the fourth Earl of Loudoun. During the excavation phase of construction, Washington's men dug up large skeletons; according to Washington, they were seven feet long.

In 1937, a site along Potomac Creek in George Washington's boyhood home of Stafford County yielded a skull "which far exceeds in brain capacity any skull previously recorded." The *Washington Post* reported:

> *A primitive Algonquin Indian who hunted and fished along the Potomac River 300 years ago and was probably a friend of the princess Pocahontas, probably was the brainiest man the world has ever seen.*
>
> *The skull of this man, which far exceeds in brain capacity any skull previously recorded, was found in Stafford County, Va., by presiding judge W. J. Graham, of the United States Count of Customs and Patent Appeals, a prominent amateur archaeologist. He announced his discovery yesterday.*

A plaque at Fort Loudoun highlighting some of the features of the fort.

Judge Graham found the skull about two weeks ago. It was in several pieces, and he sent it, as he has his other archaeological finds, to the Smithsonian Institution. There it was assembled and officials were astounded to find that it exceeds the brain capacity of any skull on record.

Judge Graham said when he saw the skull after its mounting, he was astounded. "It looked almost as big as a watermelon," he said. Its owner would have had a hat size well over eight, he estimated.

Examination of the skull shows it was healthy and not an abnormality, Judge Graham said. The skeleton of the mental giant was found, but it has not yet been assembled and measured, so the scientists do not know whether the bearer of the skull was also a man of tremendous stature. Of all the 16,000 skulls of all races of people at the Smithsonian only one approaches the capacity of Judge Graham's discovery. That is the skull of a prehistoric American found on a lonely Aleutian Island by Dr. Ales Hrdlička. It has a brain capacity of 2000 cubic centimeters.

The skull discovered by Judge Graham has a capacity of 2,200 cubic centimeters. The man who possessed it would have been a mental giant when compared with most persons today who have only 600 to 800 cubic centimeters of brain space.

Although intelligence is said to be in part dependent upon the amount of blood reaching to the brain, large brain size is also needed for great mental powers, scientists say. They point to two great men who are among those with largest brain capacity known, Napoleon Bonaparte and Count Leo Tolstoy, the Russian novelist.

The site where Judge Graham is excavating was once the village of "Patowoameke," largest Indian settlement on the Potomac. This was the way in which the Indian name for both the village and the river was originally spelled by the early explorers.

Captain John Smith visited the village and described it as a place housing about 1,500 souls.

More than 300 years ago the princess Pocahontas visited the chief of the village. It was while she was at Patowoameke that Capt. Argyle, an early explorer, kidnapped her, history declares.

Judge Graham has been interested in archaeology for many years. He has done explorations in Illinois and at Port Tobacco, Md. He published a book on his findings at the latter place.

Although it was never determined if the skull belonged to a person of great physical stature, one would have to think that such a large skull would need to be supported by a proportionally large frame. It is interesting to note that scientific papers and other writings speak extensively about archaeological finds at the site, including large ossuaries filled with human bones, but there is little to no mention of the enormous skull.

According to news reports, "the skeleton of a human being of gigantic proportions supposed to be that of a prehistoric man" was discovered in Washington County, near Bristol, in May 1906.

In Fauquier County, a mound excavation revealed "there were giants in those days." In 1866, excavators unearthed two large-statured skeletons buried with spearheads and other relics. Perhaps the most intriguing find was a "tablet containing hieroglyphics of a very curious character." Across the country, those who excavated mounds in the 1800s often found clay, stone and wood tablets with inscriptions similar to those found in Egyptian and Phoenician (and other) alphabets.

Maybe the first to mention large skeletons buried in mounds in Virginia was Swiss explorer Louis Michelle. Michelle visited the Shenandoah Valley in 1707, and local Indians showed him sacrificial altars and burial mounds of ancient warriors they claimed were over seven feet tall. This fits with later accounts, such as that from a man referred to as Captain Oliver, who found a cemetery in Shenandoah County with graves lined with stone slabs. The graves held skeletons seven feet long.

Flooding along the Shenandoah River in Clarke County unearthed mighty warriors of gigantic proportions. The *New York Times* reported the following on June 8, 1924:

> *Flood waters near Berryville, Virginia unearth a 7 1/2 foot skeleton of an ancient human. Of course, when this human, to whom the bones belonged, was alive in the flesh he would have been more like 7 feet, 9 inches tall. Also, this skeleton like some others found in the same area had generally 2 to 3 times the mass as that of contemporary humans. The grave where the skeleton was found was centrally located amongst other graves, perhaps, testifying to the important position in society that the owner of these bones once held.*

Another find, much larger than the first, was on the farm of Felix McManus, near Berryville, Virginia. This is supposed to be an old Indian cemetery, and the unearthing was done by floods when the Shenandoah River was unusually high. Practically the same sort of relics was found, including a tomahawk. The graves were grouped around a center one in which the skeleton measured seven and a half feet.

Who were these enormous people who roamed the land in the distant past? This is a question that, unfortunately, will probably never be answered. The answer will likely remain hidden—like much of Virginia's past.

"THE SOUTHERN INDIANS HAVE KILLED MY WHOLE NATION!"

I remember in my fourth grade class at an elementary school in southwestern Virginia, way back in the early 1980s, we began a new curriculum lasting six weeks or so dedicated solely to Virginia history and geography. One of the lessons was on the various Native American tribes that inhabited the commonwealth. Many folks in the region claimed a small piece of Cherokee ancestry, and the same is true for my father's side of the family. So, my friends and I were excited about this lesson—excited to learn for a change!

A couple of tribes I remember from the lesson are the Monacan and Powhatan; what I do not remember from the lesson, or any class in school for that matter, are the Senedo people. The Senedo lived along the Shenandoah

River and were all killed off between 1650 and 1700. In his 1833 work *A History of the Valley of Virginia*, Samuel Kercheval recounted the following tradition:

> *Tradition also relates that the Southern Indians exterminated a tribe, called the Senedos, on the North fork of the Shenandoah River, at the present residence of William Steenbergen, Esq., in the county of Shenandoah. About the year 1734, Benjamin Allen, Riley Moore, and William White, settled in this neighborhood. Benjamin Allen settled on the beautiful estate called Allen's bottom. An aged Indian frequently visited him, and on one occasion informed him that the "Southern Indians killed his whole nation with the exception of himself and one other youth; that this bloody slaughter took place when he, the Indian, was a small boy." From this tradition, it is probable this horrid affair took place sometime shortly after the middle of the seventeenth century. Maj. Andrew Keyser also informed the author that an Indian once called at his grandfather's, in Lancaster County, Pennsylvania, appeared to be much agitated, and asked for something to eat. After refreshing himself, he was asked what disturbed him. He replied, "The Southern Indians have killed my whole nation."*

Some believe the "Southern Indians" were the Cherokee, but others think they were the Catawba. The Catawba and Delaware tribes had been engaged in a lengthy war, and several bloody campaigns had taken place in the region, including at Antietam Creek in Maryland and Hanging Rocks in Hampshire County, West Virginia. Perhaps the Senedo broke neutrality and sided with the Delaware in some way. This might account for the ferocity of the attack and the complete lack of quarter given to the women and children.

Tribes such as the Senedo that once lived on land where subdivisions, parking lots and farms now sit came and went, and most do not know they ever existed. How many other tribes, how many other peoples have suffered similar fates not only in Virginia but also in America as a whole? Most assuredly, we are only aware of a tiny sliver of our history and of the people of yesteryear.

MOUNDS

What comes to mind first when thinking of ancient burial mounds and earthworks in North America? For many, the answer will be the aforementioned Cahokia, a six-square-mile town that contained 120 mounds, including Monk's Mound, whose base is the same size as Egypt's Great Pyramid of Giza. Others will think of the vast mounds and earthworks in the Ohio River Valley or the five-thousand-year-old Watson Brake in northern Louisiana. Few, if any, will think of Virginia in terms of mounds and earthworks. However, a number of mounds remain intact in the commonwealth, and the number that were here at one time, only to be destroyed after colonization, may exceed the wildest imagination.

The best-preserved mound in Virginia is the Ely Mound in Lee County. The mound dates to the Late Woodland–Mississippian Period (1200–1650). Lucien Carr, assistant curator of the Peabody Museum in Boston, excavated the mound in 1877. At that time, the mound was nineteen feet tall with a circumference of three hundred feet. A worker was killed during the two-week excavation, and several others were injured; no further digs have taken place since. Not far from the Ely Mound site is another mound, the Carter-Robinson Mound. Perhaps this area once held a large ceremonial complex.

In 1784, Thomas Jefferson directed the excavation of a mound near the Rivanna River in Albemarle County. In 1754, he observed local Indians conducting a ceremony in front of the mound, leading him to think it held deep significance to them and their ancestors. This was used by many as an argument against the popular notion of the day that a lost race had built the mounds.

Along the Roanoke River near Altavista is the Leesville Mound, and near the headwaters of the Rapidan River lies the Rapidan Mound. The University of Virginia conducted an excavation of the Rapidan Mound between 1988 and 1990.

Several mounds still stand in Loudoun County, one of which can be viewed off of U.S. 15 between Oatlands Plantation and the town of Leesburg. Also in Loudoun County, near the confluence of Goose Creek and the Potomac River, a mound complex was studied by archaeologists in 1994.

Where Virginia's mounds really get interesting is in the Shenandoah Valley. Here, it seems, two distinct groups of mound bounders were at work in the past. Indians from what is known as the Stone Mound Burial Culture made wide use of stone cairns in their funerary customs in the northern Shenandoah Valley. The Virginia Department of Historical Resources states the following: "One example of the great diversity can be found in the Stone Mound Burial culture in the northern Shenandoah Valley. This culture, dating from 400 B.C. to A.D. 200, placed hundreds of low stone mounds in

This mound, just south of Leesburg off U.S. 15, is one of four intact mounds in the immediate area. This mound was built between CE 1160 and 1400.

clusters on ancient bluff-like river terraces overlooking the floodplain. Only a few people were buried with great ceremony in each mound."

Sometimes, the Stone Mound people placed rare and sacred objects made from exotic materials in the graves. These objects included tubular and platform pipes, copper beads, hematite cones, pendants, basalt celts, spear-throwing stones and caches of projectile points. The people placed the objects within the mound for the deceased to use on their afterlife journeys. The few graves within each mound, the few clusters of mounds and the special objects suggest that the Stone Mound Burial culture gave only higher-ranking people this preferential treatment.

These stone cairns in the northern Shenandoah Valley are similar to those found on hillsides in West Virginia. Recently, a large complex of stone burial mounds has been found in southwestern Virginia.

Samuel Kercheval, who authored the popular *A History of the Valley of Virginia*, mentioned that there were elderly residents of the Shenandoah Valley who told him that there were many Indian mounds still standing and visible when they settled in the area. The largest was a pyramid-shaped mound near Mount Jackson that stood close to twenty-five feet in height. Sadly, the mound was destroyed during the Civil War. Kercheval discussed other large mounds throughout the Shenandoah Valley as well. For instance, Kercheval wrote: "On the land of Mr. Noah Keyser, near the mouth of Hawksbill Creek, stand the remains of a large mound. This, like that of Mr. Steenbergen's, is considerably reduced by plowing, but is yet some twelve or fourteen feet high, and upwards of sixty yards around the base."

The Seven Bends area of the North Fork of the Shenandoah River had a very high concentration of mounds, especially near the confluence of Toms Brook, but most traces today can only be seen by aerial photographs.

A TWELVE-THOUSAND-YEAR-OLD TOOL FACTORY

One of the most important—and least talked about—Paleo-Indian sites in America is the Thunderbird Archeological District in Warren County, Virginia. The district comprises several sites spanning 2,500 acres located along the South Fork of the Shenandoah River.

Thunderbird became a National Historical Landmark in 1977, due to the wealth of archaeological finds, including projectile points from the Clovis and Dalton cultures; it also possibly held the oldest structure in North America. Thunderbird is situated near jasper outcrops that served as a quarry for making tools. In fact, the quarry was an ancient tool factory of sorts for projectile points and other stone tools.

What makes Thunderbird significant is that there were permanent settlements here dating as far back as twelve thousand years. This is a drastic departure from what we have been taught—that Native Americans were largely nomadic, or at least semi-nomadic, hunter-gatherers until about three thousand years ago. In Virginia's Shenandoah Valley, at least, there were permanent civilizations in place thousands of years earlier. The Thunderbird site not only had a permanent civilization in place around the end of the last ice age, but there were also a staggering number of people living in settlements near the Shenandoah River. Along the shoals of the South Fork and near the confluence of the North and South Forks, permanent settlements have been identified that may have held up to one thousand residents.

The site is also said to have effigy mounds, including one in the likeness of a thunderbird that might be as old as twelve thousand years. There are rumors of giant burials there as well.

A subdivision now sits at an archaeological site where people from the Clovis and Dalton cultures had settlements and made tools from a nearby jasper quarry.

Today, there is a residential subdivision at Thunderbird, and only residents are permitted to drive around where excavations once took place. However, a good portion of the site is protected by an easement.

The Thunderbird site and the vast number of mounds throughout the state show that the history here was far more complex than we know. The valleys in Virginia were travel routes for many different people who hunted and traded, and some lived here for long periods of time. People came and went, and in some cases, even giants were among them, undoubtedly occupying leadership roles. What was life like long ago in the mountains and valleys of this mysterious place we know as Virginia?

7

THE MYSTERIOUS MELUNGEONS

As early as 1654, English and French explorers in the southern Appalachians reported seeing dark-skinned, brown- and blue-eyed, and European-featured people speaking broken Elizabethan English, living in cabins, tilling the land, smelting silver, practicing Christianity, and, most perplexing of all, claiming to be "Portyghee." Declared "free persons of color" in the late 1700s by the English and Scottish-Irish immigrants, the Melungeons, as they were known, were driven off their lands and denied voting rights, education, and the right to judicial process. The law was enforced mercilessly and sometimes violently in the resoundingly successful effort to totally disenfranchise these earliest American settlers.
—*N. Brent Kennedy*, The Melungeons: The Resurrection of a Proud People

In a 2014 speech addressing Muslim leaders in Latin America, Turkish president Recep Tayyip Erdogan claimed that Muslim sailors discovered the Americas long before Christopher Columbus set sail. "Contacts between Latin America and Islam date back to the twelfth century," said Erdogan, "Muslims discovered America in 1178, not Christopher Columbus." He went on to say, "Muslim sailors arrived in America from 1178." Perhaps his most shocking statement was that "Columbus mentioned the existence of a mosque on a hill on the Cuban coast."

Naturally, most were quick to dismiss Erdogan's bold claims of pre-Columbian Islamic contact in the New World; it is a radical departure from what our history books tell us. However, he may have been right.

Erdogan was echoing the words of the Islamic scholar, Dr. Youssef Mroueh, who, in 1996, wrote a paper titled "Pre-Columbian Muslims in the Americas." In it, Mroueh said, "numerous evidence suggests that Muslims from Spain and West Africa arrived to the Americas at least five centuries before Columbus." He referenced several historical documents and discussed early movements into the New World, such as this:

> *A Muslim historian and geographer ABUL-HASSAN ALI IBN AL-HUSSAIN AL-MASUDI (871–957 CE) wrote in his book Muruj adh-dhahab wa maadin aljawhar (The meadows of gold and quarries of jewels) that during the rule of the Muslim caliph of Spain Abdullah Ibn Mohammad (888–912 CE), a Muslim navigator, Khashkhash Ibn Saeed Ibn Aswad, from Cortoba, Spain sailed from Delba (Palos) in 889 CE, crossed the Atlantic, reached an unknown territory (ard majhoola) and returned with fabulous treasures. In Al-Masudi's map of the world there is a large area in the ocean of darkness and fog which he referred to as the unknown territory (Americas).*

Mroueh claimed that Ibn Farruk, a Muslim navigator, sailed into the Atlantic and stopped in the Canary Islands. From there, he headed west and saw two islands, which he named Capraria and Pluitana. This occurred in the year CE 999. Little is known about the locations of Capraria and Pluitana, but it is fair to wonder if perhaps these were the islands of Cuba and Hispaniola.

In his paper, Mroueh names other navigators who allegedly reached the Americas well before Columbus. According to Mroueh, were it not for Muslim cartographers, the Spanish and Portuguese may not have arrived in the New World when they did. The knowledge handed down from prior Muslim voyagers made it all possible.

Maybe the most persuasive argument that Mroueh presented is the names of places in the United States and Canada derived from Islamic and Arabic roots. Said Mroueh:

> *There are 565 names of places (villages, towns, cities, mountains, lakes, rivers…etc.) in U.S.A. (484) and Canada (81) which derived from Islamic and Arabic roots. These places were originally named by the natives in precolumbian periods. Some of these names carried holy meanings such as: Mecca–720 inhabitants (Indiana), Makkah Indian tribe (Washington), Medina–2100 (Idaho), Medina–8500 (N.Y.), Medina–1100,*

Hazen–5000 (North Dakota), Medina–17000/Medina–120000 (Ohio), Medina–1100 (Tennessee), Medina–26000 (Texas), Medina–1200 (Ontario), Mahomet–3200 (Illinois), Mona–1000 (Utah), Arva–700 (Ontario)…etc. A careful study of the names of the native Indian tribes revealed that many names are derived from Arab and Islamic roots and origins, i.e. Anasazi, Apache, Arawak, Arikana, Chavin, Cherokee, Cree, Hohokam, Hupa, Hopi, Makkah, Mahigan, Mohawk, Nazca, Zulu, Zuni…etc.

Skeptics are quick to point out that archaeological evidence to back Mroueh's controversial claims is scant. They may be correct; but what if the archaeological record is not where we should be looking? Instead, the best evidence might be found in the DNA of people in southwestern Virginia, eastern Kentucky, northeast Tennessee and beyond.

TURKS IN THE APPALACHIANS

There is reason to believe that the Turks beat the English, the French and perhaps even the Spanish to the southern Appalachians. When early European explorers pushed westward into the mountains, they found that isolated pockets of people were already there dwelling in log cabins. These were not Native Americans, nor were they typical Europeans; these people were called Melungeons, and they displayed characteristics of both races. Many were dark-skinned with dark hair; however, some had red hair and blue eyes. These mysterious locals spoke a broken form of Elizabethan English and practiced Christianity. Who were these people?

It was once widely assumed that the Melungeons were various tri-racial groups comprising European, African and Native American ancestry. Melungeons do indeed possess DNA from the three groups. The leading theory was that outcasts from early French, English and Spanish settlements moved into the mountains of northeast Tennessee, western North Carolina, southwest Virginia and eastern Kentucky. Runaway and freed slaves also found refuge deep in the mountains, and the two groups intermarried and also married with area Native Americans. While this scenario undoubtedly played out many times over, it is far too simplistic an explanation to fully account for Melungeon origins.

There is more to Melungeon DNA than the aforementioned African, European and Native American traits. Genetic studies show that Melungeon

This drawing, based off a photograph taken by Will Allen Dromgoole, titled *A Typical Malungeon*, appeared in the *Nashville Sunday American* on August 31, 1890. *Wikimedia Commons.*

families share traits with Mediterranean populations, those from the Middle East and even South Asia. Not all Melungeons share all of these traits; each family is unique in its ethnic history. Moreover, there may be no way to know when the various ethic components entered into a family's bloodline.

Knowing that Middle Eastern and Mediterranean DNA is present among Melungeons, does this lend credence to the idea that Muslim sailors reached the New World before Columbus? Perhaps, though the evidence is not strong. However, even if Dr. Youssef Mroueh is wrong, and there was not a pre-Columbian Islamic presence in the Americas, the existence of the Melungeons seems to prove that there were Turks in the Appalachians before the English.

Dr. Brent Kennedy, a Melungeon scholar, of Melungeon ancestry himself, believes Ottoman Turks were the first to reach Appalachia. Kennedy points to the fact that Portuguese settlers brought Turkish servants with them on their sixteenth-century voyages. Some of these may have reached American shores and headed inland, then into the mountains, and intermarried with local Native American women. Likewise, the English privateer Sir Francis Drake liberated hundreds of Turks and Moors from the Spanish in the late 1580s. Drake dropped the men on the North Carolina coast; they may have followed the same path and settled in the Appalachian Mountains.

Dr. Kennedy has found evidence for his theory in linguist connections between Turkish and Arabic words and words from Native American languages. He also claims that the term *melungeon* is derived from the Arabic *melun-jinn*, which means a "cursed soul." That the Melungeons felt themselves cursed would be evident in their very introduction into the New World as shipwrecked sailors or, worse, as slaves of the Spanish, and later in the racial prejudice they suffered in southern society.

THE DE SOTO EXPEDITION

Some believe the Mediterranean traits in Melungeon families can be traced to the Hernando de Soto expedition. De Soto is best known for being the first European to cross the Mississippi River. In fact, he died of a fever in a village on the banks of the Mississippi in 1542. In May 1539, de Soto, accompanied by a force of over six hundred men, landed on the shores of Florida. From there, the Spaniards marched through Georgia and into western North Carolina and northeastern Tennessee. This might have contributed, in a small way, to the mysterious origins of the Melungeons.

Along with the Spanish, the de Soto expedition comprised Portuguese explorers, Moors and sub-Saharan African servants. As one would expect, morale fell during the grueling expedition, and men began to desert. The highest desertion rates were among the sub-Saharan Africans and Moors.

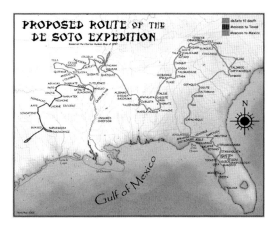

This map shows the route of the Hernando de Soto expedition that occurred between 1539 and 1543. The expedition began near present-day Port Charlotte, Florida, and de Soto died on the banks of the Mississippi River in May 1542. *Map by Herb Roe. Wikimedia Commons.*

Many of these men may have found refuge in the mountains and taken local Native American wives, giving a start to future Melungeon family lines.

The De Soto Chronicles, written in 1993 and published by the University of Alabama, is a compilation of eyewitness accounts from the De Soto expedition. It is interesting that the book gives a detailed discussion of a desertion that occurred near the present-day town of Saluda, North Carolina. The Saluda town website describes its location as "where the foothills end and the Blue Ridge begins." The *De Soto Chronicles* recounts that the expedition force held hostage a female leader from the town of Kofitachiki in present-day southeastern South Carolina. She escaped captivity with one of the African servants after pretending to need to relieve herself and failing to return. It is not hard to imagine deserters in this area heading north and settling in the historic range of the Melungeons in northeastern Tennessee, southeastern Kentucky and southwestern Virginia.

Other writings from the expedition record the desertion of a Moorish servant named Feryado and two or three other men in northwestern Georgia. Undoubtedly, there were many others whose desertions were not mentioned or who slipped away unknown. Several men were said to stay behind with native wives, and some slaves escaped with local Native American leaders. De Soto became so concerned with desertions that he threatened to hang several men.

How much the de Soto expedition contributed to the Melungeon origins is impossible to know. It is certainly reasonable to think, however, that it may have played a role.

OTHER POSSIBILITIES

There are endless possibilities when trying to pin down the origin of the Melungeons. So far, we have explored some of the more plausible scenarios. There are others that warrant mention; they run the gamut from believable to outright fanciful. The way I see things, until we have concrete answers, even the most outlandish of ideas is worthy of consideration.

One of the longest-running explanations for the origin of the Melungeons goes back to the Lost Colony of Roanoke Island. In 1587, over one hundred English settlers landed on Roanoke Island in present-day Dare County, North Carolina. Later that year, the governor of the colony, John White, returned to England for supplies. During White's absence, war broke out between the English navy and the Spanish Armada, delaying White's return to the colony. When he did arrive, in the summer of 1590, he found the colony abandoned. Everything that could be carried had been removed, and all of the boats belonging to the colony were gone. The only clue the colonists left behind were the letters "CRO" carved into a tree and the word "CROATOAN" carved into a fence post.

What happened to the colonists? Where did they go? This has been a hotly debated topic for centuries, and it seems unlikely that the mystery will be solved anytime soon. One idea, however, is that the colonists moved into the

An image from William Cullen Bryant's *A Popular History of the United States* depicting the discovery of the word *Croatoan* carved into a tree after the colony on Roanoke Island mysteriously vanished. *Internet Archive.*

An artist's interpretation of the fabled Prince Madoc leaving twelfth-century Wales for the shores of America. The drawing is found in William Cullen Bryant's *A Popular History of the United States. Internet Archive.*

interior, into present-day western North Carolina, and took up with friendly natives. This could have been the beginning of the various Melungeon bloodlines. In this scenario, at a later time, free or escaped slaves living on the frontier, away from the settlements, may have settled with descendants of the intermarriages between the lost colonists and Native Americans. Shipwrecked Portuguese sailors and the aforementioned Ottoman Turks may have even made their way into the Appalachians and settled among various groups of these isolated people, passing along their genetic traits.

Another popular notion harkens back to the supposed voyage of the Welsh prince Madoc. According to legend, Madoc sailed to America in 1170 and landed in Mobile Bay, an estuary in present-day Alabama. He and his voyagers traveled inland using various river systems and, in some cases, settled among friendly Native Americans. In other locations, they built stone walls and defensive fortifications to protect themselves from hostile tribes.

There is a plaque at Fort Mountain State Park in Georgia recounting a legend of the voyage Madoc, as well as an ancient stone wall that may have been built by the decendants of the Welsh voyagers. Some believe that earthworks along Devil's Backbone on Rose Island, about fourteen miles up the Ohio River from Louisville, Kentucky, were built by Welsh colonists. Tradition also holds that "Welsh Indians" once inhabited the island.

Members of Christopher Newport's exploratory party believed the Monacan people of Virginia spoke a language resembling Welsh. Reports of Welsh-speaking Indians also come from North Carolina. A popular notion once held that the Mandan people of the Great Plains were descendants of Madoc's Welsh colonists, as many were said to possess European features. With the varied stories of Welsh Indians, it is fair to wonder if perhaps the descendants of the fabled Prince Madoc hold a piece of the puzzle that is Melungeon ancestry.

A longshot theory, but my personal favorite, is that Carthaginians settled in the New World when their homeland fell to Rome after the Third Punic War. According to this theory, after landing in America, various groups of Carthaginians spread into the Appalachians and started the Melungeon bloodlines through intermarriages with local Native Americans.

Earlier still, the Phoenicians—the renowned seafarers who founded Carthage—may have discovered the Americas. A stone with Phoenician inscriptions was allegedly found in Brazil in 1872.

Other theories hold that the Melungeons are descended from a lost tribe of Israel that came to the Americas in the distant past. Some think bands of pirates who were active off the coast of North Carolina moved inward and settled. Each Melungeon family has its own lineage, and its origins might be a little of this and a little of that. There is probably no way to be sure of the lineage of any given family.

What we can know is that the history of America is far more complex than "in fourteen hundred ninety-two Columbus sailed the ocean blue." It is an exciting thought: pre-Columbian America, and even early colonial America, might have been every bit the melting pot that our country is today!

8

THERE'S GOLD IN THEM HILLS!

I'm an adventurer, looking for treasure.
—*Paulo Coelho,* The Alchemist

Do you like solving puzzles? If so, get out your handy decoder ring and get to work—you could be a millionaire many times over!

In 1885, James B. Ward published a pamphlet titled *The Beale Papers* that sold for 50¢ a copy (the equivalent of $13.43 today)—quite pricey for a pamphlet. *The Beale Papers* told the story of a man named Thomas J. Beale and a cache of treasure he buried in Bedford County.

The story begins in the early 1800s. According to one account, Thomas Beale fled Virginia in 1817. Those who described Beale spoke of him as a tall, ruggedly handsome man with dark hair, dark eyes and a swarthy complexion who was quite popular with the ladies. In fact, it was an argument over a woman during which Beale drew his pistol and shot a Fincastle man in the stomach that led to his fleeing the Old Dominion. In Beale's own account, he left out the argument and the shooting and claimed he headed to the western frontier with "thirty individuals of good character" on a two-year hunting expedition. The men elected Beale as their trail boss, and the adventurers from Virginia set out for the Spanish province of Santa Fe de Nuevo México.

During their adventures, somewhere in present-day southern Colorado, the Virginians came upon a mine. The group spent a year and a half extracting gold, silver and precious jewels. Beale and company made two

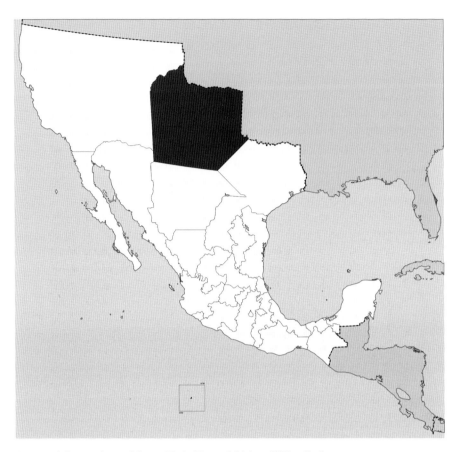

A map of the province of Santa Fe de Nuevo México. *Wikimedia Commons.*

trips back to Virginia, the first in November 1819 and the last in December 1821, and buried the treasure in a secure location somewhere near Montvale in Bedford County.

From here, the story takes an intriguing turn. Not content to draw a typical treasure map, Beale created a series of cryptograms to safeguard the loot. The first puzzle, or Paper 1, gives the location of the treasure; Paper 2 describes the contents of the loot along with other details; and the third paper lists the men in Beale's party and their relatives.

An innkeeper in Lynchburg named Robert Morriss entered the story in 1822. Beale left Morriss an iron box containing his treasure puzzles with the instructions that he should only open it if Beale or one of his men did not come to claim it after ten years. Beale went on his way back west, but a short time later, while in St. Louis, he sent a letter to Morriss.

St. Louis, Mo., May 9th, 1822

Robt. Morris, Esq.:

My Esteemed Friend:—*Ever since leaving my comfortable quarters at your house I have been journeying to this place, and only succeeded in reaching it yesterday. I have had altogether a pleasant time, the weather being fine and the atmosphere bracing. I shall remain here a week or ten days longer, then "ho" for the plains, to hunt the buffalo and encounter the savage grizzlies. How long I may be absent I cannot now determine, certainly no less than two years, perhaps longer.*

With regard to the box left in your charge, I have a few words to say, and, if you will permit me, give you some instructions concerning it. It contains papers vitally affecting the fortunes of myself and many others engaged in business with me, and in the event of my death, its loss might be irreparable. You will, therefore, see the necessity of guarding it with vigilance and care to prevent so great a catastrophe. It also contains some letters addressed to yourself, and which will be necessary to enlighten you concerning the business in which we are engaged. Should none of us ever return you will please preserve carefully the box for the period of ten years from the date of this letter, and if I, or no one with authority from me during that time demands its restoration, you will open it, which can be done by removing the lock. You will find, in addition to the papers addressed to you, other papers which will be unintelligible without the aid of a key to assist you. Such a key I have left in the hands of a friend in this place, sealed, addressed to yourself, and endorsed not to be delivered until June 1832. By means of this you will understand fully all you will be required to do.

I know you will cheerfully comply with my request, thus adding to the many obligations under which you have already placed me. In the meantime, should death or sickness happen to you, to which all are liable, please select from among your friends someone worthy, and to him hand this letter, and to him delegate your authority. I have been thus particular in my instructions, in consequence of the somewhat perilous enterprise in which we are engaged, but trust we shall meet long ere the time expires, and so save you this trouble. Be the result what it may, however, the game is worth the candle, and we will play it to the end. With kindest wishes for your most excellent wife, compliments to the ladies, a good word to enquiring friends, if there be any, and assurances of my highest esteem for yourself, I remain as ever,

Your sincere friend, T.J.B.

As is usually the case with stories such as this, the key never arrived and no one came for the box. Morriss opened the box in 1845; in addition to the cryptograms, it contained two letters from Beale. Morriss could not crack the code, and he left the box and all its contents to an unnamed friend a year before his death in 1862. The friend was able to solve the second cryptogram using the Declaration of Independence, with several words modified, as a key. The deciphered text reads:

> *I have deposited in the county of Bedford, about four miles from Buford's, in an excavation or vault, six feet below the surface of the ground, the following articles, belonging jointly to the parties whose names are given in number three, herewith:*
>
> *The first deposit consisted of ten hundred and fourteen pounds of gold, and thirty-eight hundred and twelve pounds of silver, deposited Nov. eighteen nineteen. The second was made Dec. eighteen twenty-one, and consisted of nineteen hundred and seven pounds of gold, and twelve hundred and eighty-eight of silver; also jewels, obtained in St. Louis in exchange to save transportation, and valued at thirteen thousand dollars.*
>
> *The above is securely packed in iron pots, with iron covers. The vault is roughly lined with stone, and the vessels rest on solid stone, and are covered with others. Paper number one describes the exact locality of the vault, so that no difficulty will be had in finding it.*

The weight of the gold in the treasure is 35,052 troy ounces. As of this writing, on February 9, 2021, the spot price of gold stands at $1,847.77 an ounce, making the gold worth $64,768,034.04. The spot price of silver currently sits at $27.37 an ounce. Beale's cache of silver, an incredible 61,200 troy ounces, is worth $1,675,044. Lastly, adjusting for inflation, the jewels are worth $295,633.81. These values, as high as they are, might be extremely conservative. Some have suggested that Beale and his party, rather than discovering a mine, rode through the Santa Fe province looting Spanish missions. If this is the case, the weight of the treasure would not only be in ingots and coins, but also in priceless ornaments and objects that adorned the missions. It might be impossible to place a value on the treasure.

Whatever Beale buried, even using the conservative numbers, it is still worth an amount that most would deem unthinkable. It is little wonder *The Beale Papers* have become legendary, capturing the minds of treasure hunters and puzzle solvers.

115, 73, 24, 807, 37, 52, 49, 17, 31, 62, 647, 22, 7, 15, 140, 47, 29, 107, 79, 84, 56,
239, 10, 26, 811, 5, 196, 308, 85, 52, 160, 136, 59, 211, 36, 9, 46, 316, 554, 122,
106, 95, 53, 58, 2, 42, 7, 35, 122, 53, 31, 82, 77, 250, 196, 56, 96, 118, 71, 140,
287, 28, 353, 37, 1005, 65, 147, 807, 24, 3, 8, 12, 47, 43, 59, 807, 45, 316, 101, 41,
78, 154, 1005, 122, 138, 191, 16, 77, 49, 102, 57, 72, 34, 73, 85, 35, 371, 59, 196,
81, 92, 191, 106, 273, 60, 394, 620, 270, 220, 106, 388, 287, 63, 3, 191, 122, 43,
234, 400, 106, 290, 314, 47, 48, 81, 96, 26, 115, 92, 158, 191, 110, 77, 85, 197, 46,
10, 113, 140, 353, 48, 120, 106, 2, 607, 61, 420, 811, 29, 125, 14, 20, 37, 105, 28,
248, 16, 159, 7, 35, 19, 301, 125, 110, 486, 287, 98, 117, 511, 62, 51, 220, 37, 113,
140, 807, 138, 540, 8, 44, 287, 388, 117, 18, 79, 344, 34, 20, 59, 511, 548, 107,
603, 220, 7, 66, 154, 41, 20, 50, 6, 575, 122, 154, 248, 110, 61, 52, 33, 30, 5, 38, 8,
14, 84, 57, 540, 217, 115, 71, 29, 84, 63, 43, 131, 29, 138, 47, 73, 239, 540, 52, 53,
79, 118, 51, 44, 63, 196, 12, 239, 112, 3, 49, 79, 353, 105, 56, 371, 557, 211, 515,
125, 360, 133, 143, 101, 15, 284, 540, 252, 14, 205, 140, 344, 26, 811, 138, 115,
48, 73, 34, 205, 316, 607, 63, 220, 7, 52, 150, 44, 52, 16, 40, 37, 158, 807, 37, 121,
12, 95, 10, 15, 35, 12, 131, 62, 115, 102, 807, 49, 53, 135, 138, 30, 31, 62, 67, 41,
85, 63, 10, 106, 807, 138, 8, 113, 20, 32, 33, 37, 353, 287, 140, 47, 85, 50, 37, 49,
47, 64, 6, 7, 71, 33, 4, 43, 47, 63, 1, 27, 600, 208, 230, 15, 191, 246, 85, 94, 511, 2
270, 20, 39, 7, 33, 44, 22, 40, 7, 10, 3, 811, 106, 44, 486, 230, 353, 211, 200, 31,
10, 38, 140, 297, 61, 603, 320, 302, 666, 287, 2, 44, 33, 32, 511, 548, 10, 6, 250,
557, 246, 53, 37, 52, 83, 47, 320, 38, 33, 807, 7, 44, 30, 31, 250, 10, 15, 35, 106,
160, 113, 31, 102, 406, 230, 540, 320, 29, 66, 33, 101, 807, 138, 301, 316, 353,
320, 220, 37, 52, 28, 540, 320, 33, 8, 48, 107, 50, 811, 7, 2, 113, 73, 16, 125, 11,
110, 67, 102, 807, 33, 59, 81, 158, 38, 43, 581, 138, 19, 85, 400, 38, 43, 77, 14, 27,
8, 47, 138, 63, 140, 44, 35, 22, 177, 106, 250, 314, 217, 2, 10, 7, 1005, 4, 20, 25,
44, 48, 7, 26, 46, 110, 230, 807, 191, 34, 112, 147, 44, 110, 121, 125, 96, 41, 51,
50, 140, 56, 47, 152, 540, 63, 807, 28, 42, 250, 138, 582, 98, 643, 32, 107, 140,
112, 26, 85, 138, 540, 53, 20, 125, 371, 38, 36, 10, 52, 118, 136, 102, 420, 150,
112, 71, 14, 20, 7, 24, 18, 12, 807, 37, 67, 110, 62, 33, 21, 95, 220, 511, 102, 811,
30, 83, 84, 305, 620, 15, 2, 108, 220, 106, 353, 105, 106, 60, 275, 72, 8, 50, 205,
185, 112, 125, 540, 65, 106, 807, 188, 96, 110, 16, 73, 33, 807, 150, 409, 400, 50,
154, 285, 96, 106, 316, 270, 205, 101, 811, 400, 8, 44, 37, 52, 40, 241, 34, 205,
38, 16, 46, 47, 85, 24, 44, 15, 64, 73, 138, 807, 85, 78, 110, 33, 420, 505, 53, 37,
38, 22, 31, 10, 110, 106, 101, 140, 15, 38, 3, 5, 44, 7, 98, 287, 135, 150, 96, 33, 84,
125, 807, 191, 96, 511, 118, 440, 370, 643, 466, 106, 41, 107, 603, 220, 275, 30,
150, 105, 49, 53, 287, 250, 208, 134, 7, 53, 12, 47, 85, 63, 138, 110, 21, 112, 140,
485, 486, 505, 14, 73, 84, 575, 1005, 150, 200, 16, 42, 5, 4, 25, 42, 8, 16, 811,
125, 160, 32, 205, 603, 807, 81, 96, 405, 41, 600, 136, 14, 20, 28, 26, 353, 302,
246, 8, 131, 160, 140, 84, 440, 42, 16, 811, 40, 67, 101, 102, 194, 138, 205, 51,
63, 241, 540, 122, 8, 10, 63, 140, 47, 48, 140, 288.

This cryptogram, the second of Beale's cryptic puzzles, was solved using the Declaration of Independence as a key, and it revealed the contents of the cache. *Wikimedia Commons.*

Morriss's friend had the details of the contents of the treasure, but he was unable to solve the other two puzzles and did not know where to dig. It had to be an indescribably terrible feeling. He decided to go public with what he knew and entrusted his friend James B. Ward to publish *The Beale Papers* in 1885. Ward warned those who should take up Beale's cryptograms to "devote only such time as can be spared from your legitimate business, and if you cannot spare the time, let the matter alone."

As you can imagine, countless individuals have undertaken the arduous task of trying to solve Beale's cryptograms. Those who have tried run the gamut from hobbyists to professional treasure hunters to computer programmers. Cryptographers employed by the National Security Agency (NSA) at one time took a keen interest in the mystery. The agency has declassified much of its work on the riddle.

71, 194, 38, 1701, 89, 76, 11, 83, 1629, 48, 94, 63, 132, 16, 111, 95, 84, 341, 975,
14, 40, 64, 27, 81, 139, 213, 63, 90, 1120, 8, 15, 3, 126, 2018, 40, 74, 758, 485,
604, 230, 436, 664, 582, 150, 251, 284, 308, 231, 124, 211, 486, 225, 401, 370,
11, 101, 305, 139, 189, 17, 33, 88, 208, 193, 145, 1, 94, 73, 416, 918, 263, 28, 500,
538, 356, 117, 136, 219, 27, 176, 130, 10, 460, 25, 485, 18, 436, 65, 84, 200, 283,
118, 320, 138, 36, 416, 280, 15, 71, 224, 961, 44, 16, 401, 39, 88, 61, 304, 12, 21,
24, 283, 134, 92, 63, 246, 486, 682, 7, 219, 184, 360, 780, 18, 64, 463, 474, 131,
160, 79, 73, 440, 95, 18, 64, 581, 34, 69, 128, 367, 460, 17, 81, 12, 103, 820, 62,
116, 97, 103, 862, 70, 60, 1317, 471, 540, 208, 121, 890, 346, 36, 150, 59, 568,
614, 13, 120, 63, 219, 812, 2160, 1780, 99, 35, 18, 21, 136, 872, 15, 28, 170, 88, 4,
30, 44, 112, 18, 147, 436, 195, 320, 37, 122, 113, 6, 140, 8, 120, 305, 42, 58, 461,
44, 106, 301, 13, 408, 680, 93, 86, 116, 530, 82, 568, 9, 102, 38, 416, 89, 71, 216,
728, 965, 818, 2, 38, 121, 195, 14, 326, 148, 234, 18, 55, 131, 234, 361, 824, 5,
81, 623, 48, 961, 19, 26, 33, 10, 1101, 365, 92, 88, 181, 275, 346, 201, 206, 86,
36, 219, 324, 829, 840, 64, 326, 19, 48, 122, 85, 216, 284, 919, 861, 326, 985,
233, 64, 68, 232, 431, 960, 50, 29, 81, 216, 321, 603, 14, 612, 81, 360, 36, 51, 62,
194, 78, 60, 200, 314, 676, 112, 4, 28, 18, 61, 136, 247, 819, 921, 1060, 464, 895,
10, 6, 66, 119, 38, 41, 49, 602, 423, 962, 302, 294, 875, 78, 14, 23, 111, 109, 62,
31, 501, 823, 216, 280, 34, 24, 150, 1000, 162, 286, 19, 21, 17, 340, 19, 242, 31,
86, 234, 140, 607, 115, 33, 191, 67, 104, 86, 52, 88, 16, 80, 121, 67, 95, 122, 216,
548, 96, 11, 201, 77, 364, 218, 65, 667, 890, 236, 154, 211, 10, 98, 34, 119, 56,
216, 119, 71, 218, 1164, 1496, 1817, 51, 39, 210, 36, 3, 19, 540, 232, 22, 141, 617,
84, 290, 80, 46, 207, 411, 150, 29, 38, 46, 172, 85, 194, 39, 261, 543, 897, 624, 18,
212, 416, 127, 931, 19, 4, 63, 96, 12, 101, 418, 16, 140, 230, 460, 538, 19, 27, 88,
612, 1431, 90, 716, 275, 74, 83, 11, 426, 89, 72, 84, 1300, 1706, 814, 221, 132,
40, 102, 34, 868, 975, 1101, 84, 16, 79, 23, 16, 81, 122, 324, 403, 912, 227, 936,
447, 55, 86, 34, 43, 212, 107, 96, 314, 264, 1065, 323, 428, 601, 203, 124, 95, 216,
814, 2906, 654, 820, 2, 301, 112, 176, 213, 71, 87, 96, 202, 35, 10, 2, 41, 17, 84,
221, 736, 820, 214, 11, 60, 760.

How would you like to earn over $66 million? Simply solve this puzzle, and you will have the exact location of Thomas Beale's buried treasure. *Wikimedia Commons.*

Some have gone digging for Beale's treasure. Famed treasure hunter Mel Fisher was one of the more notable folks who went after the cache. Fisher found the wreck of the Spanish galleon *Nuestra Señora de Atocha* off the Florida Keys in 1985. A hurricane had sunk the treasure-hauling vessel in 1622. It held over $450 million of gold, silver and precious stones, making Fisher a wealthy man and a celebrity in the world of treasure hunting. A fellow treasure hunter contacted Fisher about the Beale treasure, believing he had cracked the code to the first puzzle and knew the location of the loot. Fisher spent weeks digging along Goose Creek in Montvale, only to return to his Florida home empty-handed.

In 1970, Dr. Carl Hammer, director of computer sciences at Sperry-Univac, analyzed Beale's puzzles using a UNIVAC 1108 computer—a powerful, state-of-the-art piece of hardware at the time—and determined that the numbers formed an intelligent pattern rather than something haphazardly thrown together. He spent years feeding number and letter combinations into his computer, to no avail. "The computer has come up with solutions, but not the correct ones," he lamented.

The national anthem, the Magna Carta, the Bible, the text of the Louisiana Purchase, Shakespeare's plays, *Moby-Dick* and a host of other books and documents have been tried, but thus far nothing has pinpointed the loot.

Maybe that is for a good reason. The whole thing might be a hoax.

Some believe that the entire story is fake and that Thomas Beale was a fictitious character. The hoax theories range far and wide, and many sound less plausible than the story itself. Of the hoax allegations, the most believable to me is that Ward invented the story to sell pamphlets. This idea offers a simple, easy-to-believe motive, and there is evidence available to back this claim. The most compelling evidence comes from the comparison of Beale's and Ward's writings. The writing style of both men had remarkable similarities. The frequency of words appearing in the texts is striking: "I" showed up at a rate of 8.9 percent in Ward's samples and 8.7 percent in Beale's; both used "the" at a rate of 5.4 percent; "of" is 3.1 percent with Ward and 3.3 percent with Beale; and "with" came in at 1.3 percent for Ward and 1.1 percent for Beale. While "and" comprises 5 percent of most English texts, Ward used it at a 3.6 percent rate, and Beale's samples were only slightly higher at 3.7 percent. Ward averaged 2.4 commas per sentence, and Beale used 2.6. Both men used a semicolon .06 times per sentence.

The similarities do not end there. Ward's average sentence length is 28.3 words; Beale's is 29.6. The average length of words that Ward used was 4.62 letters to Beale's 4.5. As a percentage of total, conjunctions make up 5.1 percent of Ward's writings and 5.2 percent of Beale's. Ward used simple sentences 15 percent of the time and compound sentences 18 percent of the time; Beale used 16 percent and 20 percent, respectively.

These are but a few examples demonstrating the similarity in writing style between the two men; as one dives deeper into a study of the writings, even more details become apparent. English professor at the University of Kentucky Jean G. Prival, a specialist in linguistics and rhetoric, said in 1981:

> *If it is true, as many linguists claim, that any individual's writing style is characterized by idiosyncratic choice of the various syntactical options available in language, then the striking similarities in the Ward and Beale documents argue that one author is responsible for both. Although two writers might share one idiosyncratic characteristic, the sharing of several extraordinary features constitutes, I think, conclusive evidence that the same hand wrote both documents.*

No hoax or conspiracy would ever be complete without a Freemasonry angle, and with the *Beale Papers*, we have one. Ward was a master mason, and there are those who believe he invented the hoax, not to sell pamphlets, but rather, to teach a lesson. Researcher Brian Ford said the puzzle is a "brilliantly-crafted Masonic allegory that teaches its moral, not just by stating it but by having the reader pursue or be tempted to pursue an illusion."

A 1992 article in the *Washington Post* chronicled Hagerstown, Maryland resident Elwood Chaney's quest to find the Beale treasure. Chaney had a wildly different take on the matter than most—he believed the loot belonged to Quakers. Chaney postulated that Beale's hunting party was code for a band of Quakers who traveled to Africa in opposition to the slave trade. Somehow the Quakers struck it rich in Africa and used a portion of the money to help liberate slaves. The rest they brought home and hid to ensure the prosperity of their future generations. The Quakers concocted a phony story to protect the loot, which Chaney believed was buried near Hagerstown.

Others think the Beale treasure was real and that Thomas Beale did exist but that the treasure is long gone. Perhaps Bedford County residents caught wind of the treasure and dug it up. Maybe someone saw the second load of wagons come through and followed them to the spot, only to return later to claim the riches for themselves.

Some conspiracy theorists think code breakers working for the NSA solved the riddle and learned the location of the treasure. Disguised as U.S. Forest Service employees, they surreptitiously removed the loot. Perhaps, in the same way the CIA is accused of funding illegal covert operations through the drug trade, the NSA is funding secret domestic spying programs without the knowledge of Congress through the recovery of hidden treasure.

There is even a theory that at least one of the two treasure burials that Beale and his men conducted was in Bedford, Pennsylvania, not Bedford County, Virginia.

One of the more plausible notions is that Beale and his men met their end on the western plains at the hands of hostile Indians. This would explain why no one returned for the iron box and why Beale never contacted Morriss again. Then there is the idea that most of Beale's men were killed in a raid but that Beale himself and several others survived and returned to Virginia and divided the treasure. Beale did not contact Morriss—he did not need to, as he knew where the treasure was.

There is much debate as to whether Thomas J. Beale even existed, but there is no way to prove that he did not. Some say Beale had three brothers who held a combined seventeen thousand acres along the James River and

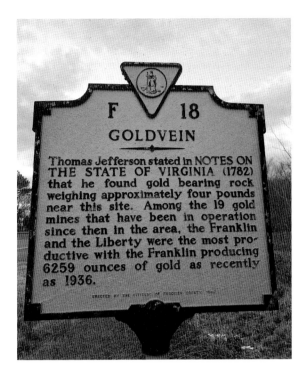

F ⧩ 18

GOLDVEIN

Thomas Jefferson stated in NOTES ON THE STATE OF VIRGINIA (1782) that he found gold bearing rock weighing approximately four pounds near this site. Among the 19 gold mines that have been in operation since then in the area, the Franklin and the Liberty were the most productive with the Franklin producing 6259 ounces of gold as recently as 1936.

ERECTED BY THE CITIZENS OF FAUQUIER COUNTY 1966

Did the same Thomas J. Beale from *The Beale Papers* have a cousin who owned a successful gold mine in Fauquier County?

owned the largest gold mine in the Blue Ridge. Interestingly, there are records of a Thomas J. Beale who was born in Fauquier County in the late 1790s. He had a cousin named William C. Beale who owned the Franklin gold mine in Fauquier County. More likely than not, this is all sheer coincidence. That said, it is fair to wonder if this Thomas Beale is the same Thomas Beale of the *Beale Papers*. If so, was William inspired to search for gold in Virginia after learning of his cousin's success in the West?

Did the treasure ever exist? If so, will it ever be found? The odds are that it will not. One would be better served panning for gold in the mountain streams on the eastern slopes of the Blue Ridge Mountains. Or, maybe better, find a place to pan for gold in the rivers that cut through Virginia's Gold-Pyrite Belt. Even the North and South Forks of the Shenandoah River will yield a little color for those patient enough to carefully sift through the sediment. Yes, panning for gold in Virginia's waterways will surely be a better use of time than trying to crack Beale's cryptograms!

— Part III —

EERIE TALES

9

THE DARK SIDE OF SHENANDOAH NATIONAL PARK

Shenandoah National Park is lovely. It is possibly the most wonderful national park I have ever been in, and, considering the impossible and conflicting demands put on it, it is extremely well run. Almost at once it became my favorite part of the Appalachian Trail.
—*Bill Bryson*, A Walk in the Woods: Rediscovering America on the Appalachian Trail

Shenandoah National Park is a gem and a natural wonder. Maybe the most amazing aspect of the pristine 311-square-mile park is that it is only 75 miles from the bustling metropolis that is Washington, D.C., and its sprawling suburbs. In 2018, 1,264,880 people visited the park, placing it among the top twenty-five most-visited national parks in America. The 105-mile Skyline Drive runs north–south through the entire length of the park and offers seventy-five stunning overlooks and access to hundreds of miles of hiking trails. The famed Appalachian Trail runs through the park, and the less-trafficked, 252-mile Tuscarora Trail begins in the park near Matthews Arm Campground. It is little wonder that folks from all over the region—and the entire nation—flock to the park, especially when the splendid fall colors are at their peak.

For its tranquil setting, crisp mountain air and endless opportunities to enjoy nature, there is another side to Shenandoah National Park—a dark side. There are rumblings of hauntings in the many family cemeteries scattered throughout the park; a haunted cabin lies deep in the forest,

The sign at the northern entrance of Skyline Drive just outside the town of Front Royal.

Looking north through Mary's Rock Tunnel, located near mile marker 32 on Skyline Drive.

This tombstone in the Fox family cemetery serves as a heartbreaking tribute to a life cut short.

A marker in the Fox family cemetery indicating that the deceased fought for the Confederacy during the Civil War.

This is all that is left of a building at the once-thriving Pocosin Mission. The mission outlived its usefulness once residents were removed from the area to create Shenandoah National Park.

The remnants of a structure still remain at the site of the former Pocosin Mission.

accessible only by foot; and ghosts wander the ridges. The slopes of the Blue Ridge have claimed a number of lives in the form of fatal plane crashes, and Skyline Drive has seen its share of deadly automobile accidents. A staggering number of suicide attempts, many of which were successful, have occurred in this otherwise serene setting, and violent crime—including a horrific double murder—has marred the mountain paradise.

Going back to the days of its inception, the formation of Shenandoah National Park was a tumultuous time that left a dark stain on our nation's history. In a gross abuse of eminent domain, the government forced residents to abandon their homes to make way for, in the words of a lobbying group in favor of the park, "a national park near the nation's capital."

A FORCED EXODUS

The establishment of Shenandoah National Park in 1926 is one of the greatest abuses of eminent domain in our country's history.
—Bart Frazier

Shenandoah National Park was established on December 26, 1935. In 1926, President Calvin Coolidge signed a bill authorizing the creation of the park, but the bill prohibited the use of federal funds for the acquisition of land. Land acquisition was the responsibility of the Commonwealth of Virginia, but the process of buying the necessary land from individual landowners was a daunting task and deemed too big of an undertaking. Said William E. Carson, director of the state commission for land acquisition: "It was manifestly hopeless to undertake to acquire the necessary area by direct purchase [because] any of the thousands of owners or claimants could hold up the entire project unless paid exorbitant and unfair prices, with jury trials, appeals, and all the endless delays which can be injected into ordinary condemnation proceedings by selfish, stubborn, and avaricious litigants."

To make it easier for Virginia to procure the land needed for the park, in 1928, the legislature passed the Public Park Condemnation Act. This bill essentially confiscated the land required to make up the park. The bill authorized $1 million to be used in conjunction with privately collected funds to compensate landowners, and a committee was formed to assess land values. The work of kicking folks out of their homes was all that remained.

A sad picture taken by Arthur Rothstein in October 1935. It is titled, "Children whose family will be resettled on new land." *Library of Congress.*

The government forced 465 families, totaling over 2,800 people, from their homes. The vast majority went without a fight. Over half the families forced out did not have legal deeds to the land that they had worked and farmed for generations. As such, only about 200 families received financial compensation. Those with cattle farms and pastures fared the best and received between $10 and $25 an acre. The government paid those with mountain lots $1 to $5 an acre. Only thirty-four landowners received more than $2,000 for their land.

About 170 families qualified for relocation assistance, and the commonwealth moved them into rambler homes in the valley. However, the resettlement homes also came with a mortgage, and within two decades, none of the original mountain families remained in the homes.

Though most of the mountain families left when the commonwealth condemned their homes, some stubbornly stayed behind and fought their evictions. Robert H. Via appealed the rulings all the way to the U.S. Supreme Court, citing the Fourteenth Amendment: "No State shall make or enforce any law which shall abridge the privileges or immunities of citizens

A picture titled *Barn and outhouses at Old Rag*, taken by Arthur Rothstein in October 1935. *Library of Congress*.

Driving along Skyline Drive, lined with thick forests, it is hard to imagine now that families who once lived here fed themselves and made money off of crops. *Library of Congress*.

of the United States; nor shall any State deprive any person of life, liberty, or property, without due process of law; nor deny to any person within its jurisdiction the equal protection of the laws." The Supreme Court declined to hear Via's case.

Lewis Willis wrote a letter to the president: "We are unwilling to part with our homes to help a small part of our population to get their hands into tourists' pockets." Of course, President Hoover was unmoved by Willis's letter, and the forced evictions continued.

H.M. Cliser sent a letter to Virginia governor John Garland Pollard in which he claimed, "I am relying wholly on the Constitution in this matter; therefore I have nothing to arbitrate." Cliser made headlines in 1935, when he sang the national anthem in protest of his eviction. The *Richmond Times-Dispatch* reported:

> *Melanchthon Cliser stood amid county officers today and sang the national anthem as he was evicted from his home near here.*
>
> *The eviction was under a court order as the State continued its efforts to move residents from the Shenandoah National Park area preparatory to its transfer to the Federal Government for park purposes.*
>
> *The eviction order signed by Grover O. Miller clerk of the Page County Circuit Court was read to Cliser by authorities.*
>
> *Following the eviction Miser was taken singing "Rock of Ages," before a judge. The judge attempted to explain why the action was necessary but Cliser refused to talk to him.*
>
> *After telling Sheriff E.L. Lucas he would make no more trouble, Cliser was released and rode in the sheriff's car to his house where a group of CCC boys assisted the officers in carrying out furniture and placing it on the highway.*
>
> *Chairman Wilbur C Hall of the Conservation Commission was said to have telegraphed park authorities from Richmond to notify Lucas to dismantle the house completely and not allow the Clisers to remain there.*
>
> *Mrs. Cliser said "I don't know what we'll do. We have no other clothes." She and her husband remained passive and gave instructions as to where their belongings were to be put.*
>
> *The work of dismantling the house was continuous tonight.*
>
> *Cliser had been fighting to keep his home on Lee Highway near Panorama since the Virginia Conservation and Development Commission started acquiring land for the park.*

He vowed he would never be removed either by force or persuasion. His 46 acres of mountain land had been condemned at a price of $4,855 set upon it, but Cliser refused to vacate.

The officers drove up to Cliser's filling station in an automobile and the elderly man came from behind his locked door and barricaded gates to serve men he thought were customers.

The deputies tarried while Cliser sang the national anthem and declared he was a free man who stood on his constitutional rather than his "shotgun" rights.

It took four deputies to force the man from the property of his father and grandfather before him.

His wife shouted after him: "Don't put up a cent of bond. You stay in jail as long as they want keep you because you're a free Man and the right is on your side."

Cliser eventually left and moved in with family who lived outside of park boundaries. He continued to fight his eviction until he died at age seventy-five.

Arthur Rothstein's 1935 picture *View of Corbin Hollow from Dicee Corbin's house. Library of Congress.*

There are other stories of folks who refused to leave and had run-ins with the law. Police dragged Lizzy Jenkins, five months pregnant at the time, out of her home and threw her belongings into a wagon. They pulled down her chimney to ensure she would have no heat for her home should she decide to stay. It was worse for John Mace. Police threw his furniture and belongings into his yard and set his house on fire as he helplessly watched.

About two dozen elderly residents were allowed to live out the remainder of their lives in their homes. The last was Annie Shenk, who moved into a nursing home in 1976. At last, no more mountain folks remained in Shenandoah National Park.

Darwin Lambert, Shenandoah National Park's first employee, who later became its historian, wrote in *The Undying Past of Shenandoah National Park*: "Removal of the mountain people, to return the land to nature's way after more than 300 years of heavy exploitation by white people was an episode rare in history. Rare, too, is the half-century regeneration of wilderness. Where else has the supposedly inevitable trend toward civility, toward more consumption of earth's resources, been so completely reversed?"

Today, driving along the breathtaking Skyline Drive, keeping a close eye out in hopes of spotting a bear, you would never know that a community of

The marker of a Confederate veteran laid to rest in the Fox family cemetery in the Shenandoah National Park.

Men from Nethers hanging out in front of the post office and general store in 1935. *Library of Congress.*

people once lived here and the government forcibly removed them from their homes. Time has forgotten them, though a faint memory of their presence lingers, as does a haunting question: Did the ends justify the means?

A HAUNTED CABIN

Nearly all the homesites and structures that lay within Shenandoah National Park boundaries were either burned or leveled—or simply left to rot as the years and the weather slowly destroyed them. That said, the authorities spared one cabin, the Corbin Cabin, located in Nicholson Hollow. George T. Corbin built the home in 1909; the government forced Corbin to vacate his property in the late 1930s, when his land was incorporated into Shenandoah National Park. The cabin was restored in 1954, and the work preserved the original character and rustic feel of the old homestead. The cabin was renovated once again in 2017. In 1989, the cabin was added to the National Register of Historic Places as the George T. Corbin Cabin.

The Corbin Cabin can be reached by the Nicolson Hollow Trail around mile marker 38 off Skyline Drive. The Potomac Appalachian Trail Club manages and maintains the cabin and rents it out at a rate between thirty and forty-five dollars a night. Should you decide to spend the night in the Corbin Cabin, you may have an encounter with a ghost. Rumor holds the cabin is haunted.

Some think the Corbin Cabin is haunted by the ghost of a woman who died giving birth to a child in 1924. Nee Corbin, the wife of George Corbin, died in the cabin giving birth to their third child, and she was laid to rest in a nearby family cemetery. Hikers who have stayed in the cabin have heard the sound of footsteps across the wood floors at night, along with other strange sounds. Many attribute the activity to Nee. Some even think she still walks the woods around the cabin.

PLANE CRASHES

A piece, albeit a small one, of the dark history of Shenandoah National Park comes in the form of deadly plane crashes, and no discussion would be complete without a mention of several of those. Henson Airlines Flight 1517 was en route to the Shenandoah Valley Regional Airport from Baltimore when it slammed into the side of a mountain within the park near Grottoes in 1985. The twin-engine, propeller-driven plane was last viewed on radar at 10:20 a.m. as it made an approach relying on its instruments, Dick Stafford, a spokesman for the Federal Aviation Administration, said. The aircraft "disappeared off radar while on approach to the airport," said Stafford, "the visibility was two miles in fog and the weather was overcast." All fourteen on board—two pilots and twelve passengers—died in the crash.

On August 24, 1994, United Press International reported that a family of five died in a plane crash in Shenandoah National Park.

The wreckage of a small plane carrying five members of an Ohio family was found on a mountainside in Shenandoah National Park in Virginia on Wednesday, and authorities said there were no survivors. Search-and-rescue teams reached the crash site early Wednesday afternoon and confirmed the plane was a Piper Cherokee that was last seen refueling in Fredericksburg, Va., on Aug. 16, said Robbie Brockwehl, park information officer at Shenandoah National Park.

Brockwehl stated, "The extreme weather at that time was definitely a contributing factor." Aboard the aircraft were forty-three-year-old pilot Bill Peoples; his wife, Mary (thirty-six); their sons, Nick (twelve) and Nate (eleven); and their daughter, Nicole (four).

In 2007, a plane bound for Georgia from Winchester crashed into a remote section of the park near Syria in Madison County. All three persons on board were killed.

The pilot of a military aircraft died during training exercises when his plane went into a dive from an altitude of 32,000 feet in October 1943. The plane crashed near Elkton and exploded on impact.

These are but a few tragedies that the mountains of the Shenandoah National Park have claimed. Other fatalities have occurred on Skyline Drive in automobile accidents. No doubt, the mountainous terrain is tricky for pilots and some drivers to navigate, and the weather quickly changes. Oftentimes, the ridges are shrouded in thick fog that reduces visibility.

DISAPPEARANCES AND DEATHS

A wilderness, in contrast with those areas where man and his works dominate the landscape, is hereby recognized as an area where the earth and its community of life are untrammeled by man, where man himself is a visitor who does not remain.
—The Wilderness Act of 1964

Every year, scores of people go missing in our national parks and national forests. In many ways, this is not only understandable, but also should be expected. Wilderness areas are fraught with danger and inherent risks. Falls, exposure to the elements and becoming lost are part of the package when exploring the wild. That said, the number of folks who disappear in these areas is astounding and disproportionate. Yosemite National Park is the leader among national parks in disappearances, but Shenandoah National Park has experienced its share as well.

Cases such as that of the discovery of the body eighty-year-old Wallace Anderson of Rappahannock County are all too common. Anderson, who often hiked in Shenandoah National Park, went missing on April 30, 2016. Over four hundred responders from forty organizations combed a one-thousand-acre area. About a week after Anderson's disappearance, searchers discovered his remains.

Of Shenandoah National Park's total area, 40 percent is designated as wilderness area, land totaling 79,579 acres. With such vast tracts of wilderness, it is no surprise that hikers routinely go missing in the park. In 2017, over eighty search-and-rescue missions took place in Shenandoah National Park, placing it in the top ten national parks in terms of such missions conducted. Deputy Chief Ranger Bridget Bohnet warned in 2016 that the park was getting more dangerous, and she attributed much of the risk to the widespread use of cell phones. She lamented that visitors to the park were not purchasing trail maps online or obtaining them at visitor centers in the park. "Instead, they're relying on navigation systems on their phones," she said. "We don't have very good coverage up here. On our entire east side there's very limited coverage."

Oftentimes, disappearances in the park, or bodies found in the park missing from other locales, is the result of foul play. In August 2018, authorities issued an Amber Alert after twelve-year-old Angie Rodriguez Rubio and her forty-eight-year-old grandmother, Elizabeth Rodriguez Rubio, went missing. Hareto Jaime Rodriguez Sariol abducted the pair in Harrisonburg on August 5; he was arrested in Pennsylvania two days later. Sariol entered a plea deal and confessed to killing Angie and her grandmother. Sariol led police to the bodies, which he had disposed of in Shenandoah County within the boundaries of Shenandoah National Park.

The world was shocked in 1996 after park rangers discovered the bodies of twenty-four-year-old Julianne Williams and twenty-six-year-old Lollie Winans in a backcountry camp near the Skyland Lodge. The pair had set out to backpack through the park with their golden retriever, Taj, less than two weeks earlier. Julie's father reported her missing on May 31, and park rangers found the victims' car north of Skyland Lodge. During the search, they found Taj walking through the park without a leash, and on June 1, they found the women's bodies.

The killer had bound and gagged both women, tortured them and slashed their throats. The depraved monster slipped off without a trace. Though the FBI and National Park Service received an estimated fifteen thousand leads, the trail was cold until a violent incident occurred in the park a year later.

In July 1997, Canadian tourist Yvonne Malbasha was riding her bicycle on Skyline Drive when Darrel David Rice ran her off the road and attempted to force her inside his vehicle. Malbasha fought him off and hid behind a tree. Fortunately, park rangers arrested Rice as he tried to exit the park. A search of his vehicle revealed Rice had hand and leg restraints with him. In 1998, Rice pled guilty to the attempted kidnapping, and the court sentenced him to 135 months in federal prison.

Rice later became a suspect in the murders of Julianne Williams and Lollie Winans, and video footage found that he entered the park in 1996 on May 25, May 26 and June 1. He was indicted for the murders in 2001, but in 2003, authorities tested a hair found at the scene which did not belong to either of the victims or Rice. The case against Rice fell apart, and prosecutors dismissed the charges without prejudice.

The hunt continues to this day for the killer of Julianne Williams and Lollie Winans. In 2016, the FBI issued a statement asking the public for help solving the crime:

> *Special Agent in Charge Adam S. Lee of the Richmond Division of the FBI wishes to bring attention to the murders of Julianne "Julie" Williams and Laura "Lollie" Winans in the Shenandoah National Park 20 years ago.*
>
> *Julie and Lollie had been hiking with their dog, Taj, and were last seen on May 24, 1996. After Taj had been found wandering the Park he was turned over to Park Rangers near the Whiteoak Canyon Trail and a search ensued. The bodies of both women were found on June 1, 1996, at their campsite near Skyland Resort in the Shenandoah National Park.*
>
> *At the time of their deaths, the ladies were:*
>
> *Julianne Williams*
> *Age 24*
> *Height 5'9"*
> *Weight 125 lbs*
> *Hair: Brown—medium length*
> *Race: white*
>
> *Laura Winans*
> *Age 26*
> *Height 5'8"*
> *Weight 160 lbs*
> *Hair: Light brown—long length*
> *Race: white*
>
> *The National Park Service and the FBI have investigated this case for years, and it very much continues to be an active, ongoing investigation. Investigators wish justice for Julie and Lollie, and closure for the Williams and Winans families. In that vein, the FBI has generated updated posters seeking information about this double murder and encourages the public to*

contact authorities with any information that may lead to the identification of the person or persons responsible. The public is requested to share this release and attached posters with friends, family, coworkers and social media contacts in an effort to bring national attention to this investigation and appeal to someone to call authorities with what may wind up being the critical piece of information needed.

The Blue Ridge Parkway, a scenic stretch of mountainous road connecting Shenandoah National Park in Virginia and Great Smoky Mountains National Park in North Carolina, has experienced a staggering number of homicides over the years. Recently, a road-rage shooting occurred, which seems unthinkable on the picturesque highway dubbed "America's Favorite Drive."

A man from Sweden was found shot to death along the parkway in 1994. In 1997, a woman and her five-year-old son were found stabbed to death. In 1998, a shirtless man holding a beer in one hand and a rifle in the other shot and killed Ranger Joe Kolodski. Police discovered the dismembered remains of a local farmer in 2004; his remains were scattered about the parkway. In 2006, about six months apart, a male homicide victim and a twenty-two-year-old woman were found along the roadway. In 2010, the body of a murdered man was discovered, and later that year, a gunman shot and killed a man and wounded his female companion while they sat at an overlook. Seth Willis Pickering stabbed his six-year-old daughter to death on the parkway and received a life sentence for the atrocity. Twenty-nine-year-old Sara Ellis was killed in 2018; an autopsy revealed she died of strangulation and suffered blunt force injuries to her head, chest, arms and legs.

Though areas such as the Blue Ridge Parkway and Shenandoah National Park are statistically as safe as anywhere in the country, the violent crimes that have occurred are enough to give one pause about visiting. Moreover, the Appalachian Trail, running from Maine to Georgia, which cuts through Shenandoah National Park and Blue Ridge Parkway, has experienced eleven murders since 1974. It is unsettling to know that even these tranquil settings are not enough to keep out the evil of the world.

What might be even more shocking than homicides on the Blue Ridge Parkway and Shenandoah National Park are the astonishing number of suicides. In 1996, James S. Schneider, age twenty-seven, was found dead in Shenandoah National Park of a self-inflicted gunshot wound. In 2011, a woman killed herself by driving her vehicle off Skyline Drive. She died from her injuries after her vehicle plunged five hundred feet down a steep slope.

In 2013, twenty-one-year-old Tyler Keefer died from suicide on the Dickey Ridge area of Shenandoah National Park. Fairfax County firefighter Nicole Mittendorff, age thirty-one, took her life in the park in 2016; authorities found her remains near the Whiteoak Canyon Trail parking area.

In 2018, there were an astonishing ten suicides on the Blue Ridge Parkway. The Centers for Disease Control noted that between 2003 and 2009, the Blue Ridge Parkway and Shenandoah National Park ranked first and seventh, respectively, among all national parks in the number of suicides. During that period, there were fifteen suicides, along with six attempts, on the Blue Ridge Parkway, and three suicides and five attempts in Shenandoah National Park. Why? What is it about these places that draw desperate people who feel taking their own lives is their only option?

Perhaps the most notable suicide in Shenandoah National Park is that of Roy Cleveland Sullivan. Sullivan was born in 1912 in Greene County, Virginia, and he became famous for being struck by lightning more than any person on record. As a child, lightning struck Sullivan's scythe as he helped his father clear a field. He escaped injury and went on to be struck by lightning seven more times between 1942 and 1977 while working as a park ranger in Shenandoah National Park. Sullivan earned the nicknames "Spark Ranger" and "Human Lightning Rod" and is even recognized by Guinness World Records as the person struck by lightning more recorded times than anyone else. He did not claim his lightning strike as a kid, since it could not be confirmed; officially, he survived seven lightning bolts rather than eight. The odds of any one person being hit by lightning seven times in their life are estimated to be about 4.15 in 100,000,000,000,000,000,000,000,000,000,000.

Alas, Sullivan did to himself what lightning could not do. On September 28, 1983, he died after having shot himself—at least officially. Some believe Sullivan was a victim of foul play. He supposedly shot himself while lying in bed next to his wife, and miraculously, the gunshot did not awaken her. He allegedly fired the shot at 3:00 a.m., but his wife did not report the death until 9:00 a.m. Moreover, family members claimed the couple was having marital troubles at the time of his death.

Today, Sullivan's memory lives on in the record books, and he is remembered by the Department of the Interior as the "Chuck Norris of park rangers." It is sad to think how tragically his life ended.

For all of Shenandoah National Park's natural splendor, magnificent overlooks, stunning waterfalls and the solitude of its wilderness areas, an air of melancholy surrounds it. The residents forced from their land and those

The "Spark Ranger," Roy Sullivan, holding a hat he wore when a lightning bolt struck him. *Department of the Interior*.

who have ended their lives prematurely have left an indelible impression on the park. I am remined of the words Mark Frost penned in *Twin Peaks: The Final Dossier*: "There is no light without darkness—and this troubles many of us—but without it, how else would we tell one from the other? We spend half of every day in darkness; surely we should make our peace with this."

10

A VIRGINIA GHOST TOWN

*There is something ineffably sad about a ghost town. Imagination pictures the
everyday life of the vanished people—their joys and sorrows, their aspirations and
pastimes. When human beings abandon a dwelling they inevitably leave behind some
shreds of their own personalities; and a deserted city has a melancholy so powerful
that the least sensitive visitor is impressed by it.*
—*Percy Fawcett,* Exploration Fawcett: Journey to the Lost City of Z

During its existence, Virginia has lost a great portion of its land.
After all, Virginia's territory once extended as far north as the
Great Lakes and west to the Mississippi River. As time went on,
the states of Illinois, Indiana, Kentucky and, most recently, West Virginia,
were carved from the Old Dominion. Even a sliver of western Pennsylvania
once belonged to Virginia—the "Lost County of Yohogania."

Yohogania County lay in a region where Virginia and Pennsylvania had
a long-standing border dispute. During the 1780s, a new boundary survey
resolved the disagreement when it determined that the bulk of Yohogania
County lay inside Pennsylvania's borders. Legislators created new boundaries,
and a piece of land in the present-day West Virginia panhandle went to
Virginia; the rest went to Pennsylvania and became today's Westmorland
County and parts of Fayette, Washington, Allegheny and Beaver Counties.

Country, state, county and town boundaries change over time; this is the
natural order of things as populations shift and those in charge redraw the

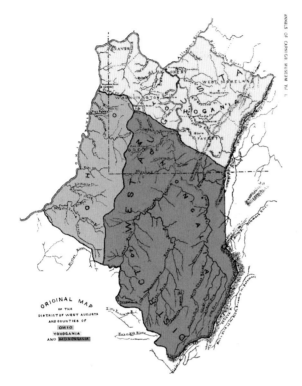

A map of Map of Ohio, Monongalia and Yohogania Counties in the 1700s. Yohogania County is the northernmost county on the map. *Wikimedia Commons*.

lines on our maps. In some cases, however, towns up and disappear, and population centers are abandoned, leaving a void on the map and only a faint memory of their existence. This occurred in Lignite, Virginia.

LIGNITE

Lignite, Virginia—population: zero.

Tucked away in the Jefferson National Forest in Botetourt County lie the remains—what little are left—of a once-thriving mining town. Lignite takes its name from the shabby, inferior brown coal found in the region, but Lignite was actually an iron-mining town established in 1899 by the Alleghany Ore and Iron Company (now Lukens Steel Company).

The town of Lignite sat on about seventy-five acres, and the entire mining complex spanned approximately two hundred acres. About three hundred laborers and their families lived in the town, which had its own post office, theater, school, church and, of course, company store. Roads from the towns of Eagle Rock and Oriskany ran to Lignite, and rail cars carried iron ore out of town.

Botetourt County was a hub for iron mining in the early twentieth century. Allegheny Ore and Iron Company, which became a subsidiary of Lukens Steel Company in 1907, and its mine in Lignite had local competition, including a nearby rival in the Low Moor Iron Company. Both companies were reliant on cheap labor. U.S. Forest Service archaeologist Mike Barber said the Lignite operation "was basically an iron plantation." Workers in Lignite mined the ore, "busted it up, washed it and railed it out of here," according to Barber.

As an example of how low wages were for iron miners in the early 1900s, the Low Moor Iron Company paid workers at its Kay Moor mine, in Fayette County, West Virginia, an average of $36.26 per month. The company issued half its workers' pay in scrip, to be used in exchange for goods and services—provided by the company, of course. Workers in those days surely did owe their souls to the company store, as the old song goes.

Few today know that Lignite ever existed. It is as if the town suddenly sprang up, only to disappear almost as fast, leaving only the haziest of memories behind. Perhaps Lignite would have been forgotten altogether were it not for a stroke of dumb luck. In the spring of 1998, the U.S. Forest Service conducted a controlled burn that cleared away thick undergrowth and revealed the remains of the lost town. The forest service, along with students from James Madison University in Harrisonburg, collected artifacts and mapped the town.

So, what happened to Lignite?

It goes without saying that mining is a tough business. The industry is prone to boom-and-bust cycles; companies face tough competition and deal with razor-thin profit margins and ever-changing regulations. Sometimes, the deposits run out. In the case of Lignite, however, the company abandoned the site after finding a better and more profitable vein in Pennsylvania in the early 1920s. The company dismantled many of the structures in town and sold them for building supplies, and the miners and their families left and sought employment elsewhere. After a couple of decades, Lignite was no more.

Although the company pulled up stakes and the miners and their families abandoned the town, Lignite did not die overnight. It took about twenty-five years for the town to completely perish and make its transition into a true ghost town. Local stories tell of people coming to Lignite after its abandonment and claiming empty homes for themselves. These squatters stayed until about 1950, when the government forced out the last of the

The drive down the rutted and narrow dirt road to Lignite is somewhat eerie on its own. It is even more so when the locals post signs such as this.

occupants. At that point, like an episode from History Channel's *Life after People*, the forest began the process of reclaiming the town.

From forest to bustling iron-mining town, and back to forest again. Ashes to ashes, dust to dust. All in a manner of decades—and barely anyone noticed.

I visited what is left of Lignite in December 2019. I reached the town by turning onto Route 704 from Craig Creek Road. There is no quick way to get there; going to Lignite requires a lot of driving along backroads until finally coming to a narrow, rutted dirt road that leads to the old town. Lignite has a creepiness about it. Adding to the feeling of uneasiness, about half a mile from the old town, an unwelcoming sign nailed to an old post along the road reads: "Warning: If you can read this, you are in range." For full effect, the sign has a set of crosshairs on it. I brushed off the sign as I drove by, thinking that it had to have been placed there by someone trying to be funny. At the same time, I knew I would hate for my car to break down on that lonely road late at night.

The town of Lignite is a mile off Craig Creek Road. A weathered brown sign points the way. But once you have driven a mile, there is nothing indicating you are there. As I reached what should have been my destination, I remember wondering if I had arrived or if Lignite was farther down the road, or if there was even anything at all to see. I saw nothing that indicated I was in a ghost town—no buildings or billboards, no rusted automobiles, and there were certainly no blowing tumbleweeds, as in the movies. But as luck would have it, about the time I was kicking myself for spending the morning driving all the way to Lignite, I saw a couple of foundations in the woods.

The remains of the foundation of a house in the old mining town of Lignite.

A piece of a foundation of a house with a protruding rusty metal pipe is an eerie reminder in the middle of the forest that a thriving town once stood here.

Bottles, chunks of glass, bricks and pieces of steel litter the forest floor where the town of Lignite stood.

I parked my car and spent several hours exploring what little is left of Lignite—which isn't much. Pieces of house foundations are scattered about, and piles of bricks litter the woods. Rusted-out galvanized steel tubs, broken glass and cans and rusty pieces of steel are all that is left to tell the story of the old company town. As I walked along a small creek that cut through the woods, I imagined children throwing rocks and splashing around, having fun playing here a century ago. I wondered what it was like to be a kid growing up in this company town.

The most visible remains of Lignite are two chimneys in an overgrown field strangled by vines and briars. Thorns tore at my clothes and exposed skin, and the vines wrapped around my feet and legs, trying their best to trip me as I walked to chimneys. This spot was once the nicest home in town; it was a mansion where the mine manager lived. Naturally, squatters were quick to occupy this home after the company left for more profitable ventures in the Keystone State.

The outlines of old roads crisscross the woods where streets once lay, and paths that I surmised must have been used to transport iron ore led deeper into the woods outside the town's center. Rusty rocks containing iron ore lie all over the woods, from small to boulder size, and old mining pits can be found all over.

These two chimneys, remnants of the mine manager's mansion, choked in weeds and undergrowth, are the most visible reminder of the town of Lignite. Clearly, the forest is reclaiming the land where a town once stood.

Rusty rocks and boulders containing iron can be found all over the woods around the former town of Lignite.

Pieces of iron ore ranging in size from pebbles to boulders are scattered about the forest floor in Lignite.

I was upset with myself as I walked along exploring the old foundations of the former town. I meant to bring my electromagnetic frequency (EMF) meter to see if I could pick up any spikes (possibly indicating the presence of paranormal activity) around the old homesteads. Unfortunately, I was half asleep as I loaded the car for the trip, and my meter was sitting in my office while I explored Lignite. But that's okay—I didn't need it. You can feel the presence of those who toiled in the iron pits a century ago and almost hear children playing in the dusty streets. A heavy desperation still hangs in the air from the poverty-stricken mountain folks who moved into the abandoned houses and from the overworked, underpaid and scarcely fed miners and their families. Lignite may be gone, but something of the people still remains.

A DEAD INDUSTRY

You would never know it now, but Virginia was once home to a thriving iron industry. It is estimated that the commonwealth produced $317 million in pig iron between 1830 and 1930. Pig iron is crude iron that requires additional processing, so named because of the molds used during production. The molds had a central channel with many individual ingots running off of it resembling a sow nursing a litter of piglets.

Iron production in Virginia began during the early colonial period using bog iron. However, most of Virginia's furnaces and mining operations took place in western Virginia, with a high concentration of furnaces in the Shenandoah Valley. The most profitable days of Virginia's iron industry were between the 1820s and 1850s, but as the 1850s approached, more efficient furnaces in Pennsylvania that burned anthracite coal, rather than charcoal, put many of Virginia's furnaces out of work until the ovens were ramped up again during the Civil War.

Virginia experienced a resurgence in iron production in the early 1900s, but by the 1940s, the Old Dominion had produced its last iron ingot. Today, all that is left of the iron industry are furnaces scattered throughout the mountains and faint memories of old iron towns.

One such town was Spec, another of Botetourt County's iron towns. Southeast of Lignite, across I-81 along the Blue Ride Parkway, you will find the Iron Mine Hollow Overlook. Down below lies the unincorporated town

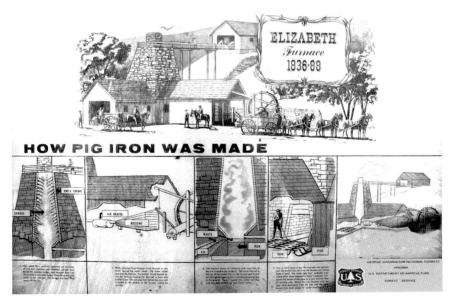

A display at the Elizabeth Furnace Recreation Area in the George Washington National Forest in Shenandoah County. *U.S. Forest Service.*

Roaring Run Furnace, in the Jefferson National Forest in Botetourt County, is a reminder of Virginia's days of iron production.

Roaring Run Falls is located in the Jefferson National Forest in Botetourt County, north of the town of Eagle Rock. The falls are located upstream of a nineteenth-century iron furnace.

A piece of specular hematite, from which the town of Spec, Virginia, took its name. *Wikimedia Commons*.

(if you can even call it a town) of Spec. Spec was named after the region's specular hematite, and a century ago, the town was an iron hub. Spec was a company town that was reduced to nothing after the company fell on hard times and pulled out.

While Spec does not qualify as a ghost town in the same way as Lignite, it suffered a similar fate. In 1920, the Pulaski Iron Company purchased a large tract of land for mining operations and built a powerhouse, washer and tipper alongside the railroad tracks. The company had about twenty-five employees on-site, and it built houses for the miners and their families.

The mining operation at Spec was profitable, but only for a short time. By the late 1920s, mining ceased at Spec, and the Pulaski Iron Company left town. All that is left today are some foundations and the old brick powerhouse. Like Lignite, Spec came and went, and few knew when it was gone.

Spec Station along the Norfolk & Western Railroad in 1927. Shown are the Pulaski Iron Company's tipple and crusher, where hematite from the nearby mine was loaded onto rail cars. *U.S. Geological Survey.*

These have been just a few tales of boom and bust years, company towns and entire industries that came and went, leaving little behind to remind us of the boom years. What industries will fail in the future? Which towns deep in the mountains of Virginia will be reclaimed by the forest one hundred years from now, and who will tell their stories? Only time will tell.

11

UFOs AND ALIENS

Two possibilities exist: Either we are alone in the Universe or we are not.
Both are equally terrifying.
—Arthur C. Clarke

Toward the end of 2019, I saw dozens of news reports of "snakelike" UFOs in the United States. The highest concentration of these anomalous aerial objects seemed to be in Texas. One night, a Twitter follower mentioned me and several others in a post with a link to a news article about these objects. I read the piece, plus several others, and the following morning, I sent a link in a text to my sister that read, "Look familiar?"

Minutes later, she responded, "Yes!" She went on to recount familiar motions of the objects in question, saying, "The tilting back and forth is what I experienced, too!"

To give some background, these snakelike UFOs are weird objects with a "dull metal color" and resemble a large "black pipe" hovering in the sky. They move and tilt in a way that is unlike any conventional aircraft. Some witnesses claim that these things "snake their way" across the sky.

This current rash of sightings came to light when a YouTuber in California captured footage of a snakelike object moving through the sky over the Mojave Desert in June 2019. Since then, the objects have been spotted everywhere, with the number of reports reaching into the hundreds—that we know of. What is more, many UFO researchers believe that the U.S.

government is not only aware of these snakelike UFOs but also keeping close tabs on them.

Although the snakelike UFOs seem to be a recent phenomenon within the world of ufology, they have been around for an indeterminate amount of time. In fact, my sister saw one hovering over the town of Front Royal on a summer morning in 2017.

I was at work, and my phone buzzed sometime after ten o'clock. I picked it up and saw a text with a strange picture from my sister. I don't remember exactly what I texted back to her, but it was something along the lines of: "What the hell is that?"

She responded back immediately: "Right?"

I studied the picture; it was nothing I had ever seen before. It looked like a large black pipe suspended in the air. The first thought that came to mind was a description I had read in countless UFO reports: "cigar-shaped" object.

We sent one another a barrage of text messages, and I went on to say, "That's a freaking UFO!" We continued to text back and forth most of the day, and I was consumed by her encounter—completely shocked. I have to admit, too, that I was a little jealous.

There are a couple of things I should mention regarding the sighting. The first is that my sister is in no way a paranormal enthusiast. Unlike her older brother, she does not immerse herself in UFO lore or search the skies for anomalous aerial objects. She does not hunt ghosts or go tromping through the forest looking for Bigfoot in her spare time. In other words, she does not do any of those things that I do or care about the things that fascinate me. So, she does not bring any inherent biases or the predisposition to believe in the fantastic to the table. Second, my sister is a former police officer. She is not prone to exaggeration and has been trained to report her observations in great detail, even when under duress. That adds additional weight to her report, in my opinion.

Later that night, I urged her to file a report with the Mutual UFO Network (MUFON), and I sent a link to the reporting form on its website. I told her the likelihood of her case being solved was slim to none—and Slim had left town—but nevertheless, it would be a positive thing for a group engaged in the collection of UFO data to have a record of her encounter on file. A few days later, she filed her report and later spoke with an investigator over the phone. Her case is no. 85373. The following is a synopsis.

A snakelike UFO spotted by the author's sister in Front Royal in 2017.

On 7/19/17 at 10:15 AM the witness was driving to a Dr. Appointment in Front Royal, VA when the witness saw a cigar shaped object in the sky. The witness noted it hovered in place and the only movement was from a Horizontal to Vertical position in a very slow turn. The witness observed the object for 5 minutes until the witness's destination. The witness took 3 photos and then took 30 seconds to get the kids out of the car to see the object and it was gone.

The investigator concluded that whatever my sister saw was "not a natural phenomenon or a man-made object." He went on to say, "The craft that the witness observed is an Unidentified Flying Object of unknown origin."

Interestingly, on the same day as my sister's sighting, a nearly identical object was spotted in Buckingham County, about one hundred miles south of Front Royal. With the recent wave of "snakelike" UFOs sweeping the

The author and several family members testing a large solar balloon to see if it could explain his sister's UFO sighting.

nation, I view the Buckingham County and Front Royal sightings in the summer of 2017 as a precursor to the current phenomenon.

I investigated the site where my sister saw the UFO and thoroughly questioned her. I then set out to try and debunk the sighting. The only thing I could come up with that might have been similar was a large, black solar balloon. So, a few weeks after the encounter, she and I, along with several family members, met up at a park and tested a solar balloon. We had a lot of fun with the experiment, and my young nephews enjoyed handling the enormous balloon. But at the end of the day, she said, "That thing is really cool, but that's not it." She went on, "I don't know what I saw, but it wasn't that!"

THE WYTHE COUNTY UFOs

There are two types of UFOs—the ones we build and the ones "they" build.
—Ben Rich

On October 7, 1987, three Wythe County sheriff's deputies, all former members of the military, told the sheriff they had spotted an unidentified flying object. Local radio reporter at WYVE, Danny Gordon, learned of the story from the sheriff and decided to run it as a filler piece at the end of the newscast—a light-hearted, funny piece. Gordon related the following:

> *It was a filler piece that came on at the end of the news which I usually relegate to something that's maybe unusual, like we had one police officer who killed five chickens at once with two shots, and that was a story that ran as kind of a "ha ha" piece, and this was another "ha ha" piece and being a very skeptical newsman, it was definitely not in my lead part of my news.*

Little did Gordon know at the time, but his offbeat story would hit a nerve in the local community. The report set off a flurry of calls to the station, and a flood of UFO sighting reports came in—so many, in fact, that Gordon scheduled a call-in show for listeners to discuss their encounters.

Gordon was of the mind that the military was the culprit behind the spate of UFO sightings. "It appears we are dealing with something of a military nature." He implored the military to come clean: "A lot of people are scared; will the military please tell us where they are?"

Gordon contacted the military on several occasions, and they assured him no testing of experimental aircraft was taking place in Wythe County. They did offer an explanation: planes refueling. This explanation, however, did not hold up. Said Gordon:

> I called the Pentagon and talked to the Air Force General there, who told me if they're refueling under 13,000 feet, then somebody's butt's in a sling. And to this day, we don't know if they were refueling at 5,000 feet. But at the same time, I have asked, if it is military, then I'll back off the story and leave it alone if you tell me because I'm a patriot. And each time I'm told it's not us, we're not doing it, and we haven't been doing it.

On October 21, Gordon had a UFO encounter of his own. He and his friend Roger Hall, a commercial pilot, drove to an area in the county where the bulk of sightings had taken place. After a fruitless two-hour stakeout watching the skies, they left. However, on the way home, they spotted a wingless, dome-shaped object in the sky with colored lights. Gordon pulled the car over, and both men exited the vehicle and watched the anomalous craft. Gordon said: "As I watched the sky, from the left came the red ball. As the big mothership went into a small skiff of clouds, the red ball docked with the craft." Unfortunately, the pair got so caught up in the moment that they forgot to photograph the object.

Gordon and Hall went back out the following night in search of UFOs, and this time, they got the pictures they were after. However, after the pictures were developed, they were disappointed—the photographs showed only ambiguous streaks in the night sky.

Gordon called a press conference to address the UFO flap, and this must have rubbed some people the wrong way. The night before the event, he received a phone call from an unidentified man who told him "to be aware that the CIA and federal government were very much interested in the Wythe County UFOs." He received other anonymous phone calls telling him it was "not his place to be messing around in defense matters."

After the press conference, when Gordon arrived at his home, someone had broken in. Nothing was missing, but he was convinced the intruders were after the UFO photos that he took while out with Roger Hall.

UFO sightings in Wythe County continued at a dizzying pace. By December, Gordon had received over 1,500 reports. After an eighteen-month period, there were over 3,000; that is when he stopped counting. Though that is a staggering number of reports, it goes without saying that the vast majority of UFO sightings go unreported. Taking that into account, it is truly remarkable what was happing in the skies over Wythe County in the late 1980s. Gordon said that people from all walks of life were seeing the objects, and many were the kind you would not expect—veterans, politicians and a former town mayor, to name a few.

As UFO sightings continued, so did Gordon's harassment. On March 19, 1988, he was packing for a broadcaster's conference in Virginia Beach, where he was scheduled to speak on the Wythe County UFO sightings. He received a disturbing phone call from a man claiming to be a former military intelligence officer. The voice on the other end told Gordon to tape the conversation, saying, "I want your friends to know, that if something happens to you, that I forewarned you." He said the stranger made a bizarre and chilling accusation against the government: "He told me that because of his investigations into the UFO field that they had hit his son and caused his son to die with some kind of virus connected to leukemia. He said that he had information that the federal government was not very happy with my UFO investigations."

Things got worse. Not long after the former intelligence officer contacted Gordon, two strange men came to his home. They claimed to be newspaper reporters and spent about forty-five minutes with him. Strangely, only one of the men conducted the interview while the other walked throughout the house taking pictures. They promised to send Gordon a copy of the article they were working on, but they never did. He called the newspaper and learned neither man was employed there.

A few weeks after this bizarre incident—to a student of UFO lore, it sounds eerily similar to a meeting with the storied "Men in Black"—Gordon discovered that a negative of a UFO photograph he had shot at a nearby shopping mall was missing from a canister containing several other negatives.

All of the stress from the UFO craze took its toll on Gordon and his family. Out of fear, and for the sake of their mental health, his wife and daughter left their home and moved in with his mother-in-law. Later, Gordon's wife rushed him to the emergency room after he keeled over. Doctors hospitalized him. The stress and exhaustion from his involvement with the wave of UFOs had wrecked his health.

If Gordon could go back in time and do things over again, he would steer clear of the UFO topic. "If I had my choice, I'd not report the UFO story again. It's just been too hard on my life and created too many problems." He gave a simple warning to others: "Don't look up." Gordon later penned a book with that same title.

Over thirty years have passed since Wythe County became ground zero for a wave of strange objects zooming through the sky. Was the government testing experimental aircraft? Did someone choose Wythe County as the location for a psychological warfare experiment? Was it aliens? No one knows and probably never will. The UFO wave of the late 1980s has largely been forgotten—except by those who saw something and the ones whose lives were forever changed by the events.

CLOSE ENCOUNTERS

Why should it be more difficult for us to accept encounters with "creatures" than with "craft"? Probably because once we dare to admit that beings alien to ourselves exist, we are forced to face our deepest fear of the unknown, along with our more basic and specific fears of competition and hostility.
—Dr. J. Allen Hynek, The Hynek UFO Report

The legendary UFO investigator and researcher J. Allen Hynek—those unfamiliar with his books might remember him from History Channel's fictional series *Project Blue Book*—established a six-item classification system for UFO reports in his 1972 book *The UFO Experience: A Scientific Inquiry*. This became known as the Hynek Scale. I summarize the scale as follows:

1. Nocturnal lights. This category comprises the bulk of UFO reports and represents lights in the sky, often colored, that move in a strange way.
2. Daylight disks. These would be your "flying saucer" reports—metallic, disk-shaped objects that move at incredible speeds. Other daytime UFOs would fit here, too, such as cigar-shaped objects.
3. Radar visuals. These are anomalous radar blips. Sometimes, these correspond to anomalous lights or daytime disks.
4. Close Encounters of the First Kind (CE-I). This is when a UFO is spotted within two hundred yards of a person and the witness is able to make out some details. The UFO in these cases does not interact with witnesses or the environment.
5. Close Encounters of the Second Kind (CE-II). In these cases, the UFO has some sort of physical effect on the environment and/or witnesses. Examples include, but are not limited to, scorching the ground or trees; frightening animals, perhaps having a negative effect on the milk production

of a cow; interfering with the electrical systems of automobiles; and witnesses suffering from conjunctivitis or becoming ill after the encounter.
6. Close Encounters of the Third Kind (CE-III). This category was made famous by the Steven Spielberg movie of the same name. Hynek was a consultant for the film and made a cameo appearance. A Close Encounter of the Third Kind is when an entity is present in or near the UFO. The entities may be human, humanoid or robots who seem to be occupants or pilots of the UFO.

Some have argued for more types of close encounters, though these are not widely accepted in the same way as Hynek's categories, due to their lack of scientific rigor. The most popular additional category is the Fourth Kind, in which an abduction occurs. Some believe nonabduction cases should be added to the Fourth Kind when hallucinatory or dreamlike states are attributed to UFO encounters. Other additional categories include the Fifth Kind, when alleged direct communication occurs between witnesses and extraterrestrials; the Sixth Kind, when a human or animal is killed during a UFO encounter; and the Seventh Kind—perhaps the most bizarre of all—when a human/alien hybrid results from a UFO encounter.

Clearly, various reports during the Wytheville UFO flap in the late 1980s met the criteria for several of Hynek's categories. Although they are not disklike, the snakelike UFOs mentioned earlier would fall into Hynek's daylight disk category. Some of these may qualify as a CE-I if the witness was close enough to the object.

A CE-II occurred in Lynchburg in 2010. According to the witness statement in MUFON case no. 21863:

I was taking my daughter home after work on this evening. It was about 11:00 at night and we were sitting by her mailbox when we noticed lights down the road towards the rental property she lives in on a farm here. The lights were small, much like backup lights on a car, so we just thought that it was her landlords working on a farm truck. We sat by the mailbox and waited a minute or so for them to come out of the road. When after a few minutes, the lights were still there, I pulled my car up closer to the lights. As we approached them, they backed up into the hayfield. I had my car window rolled down to listen, at the neighbors entrance, the first on the road is where the lights were first on the ground and their dogs were barking and crying and howling! We didn't hear any motor noises from the farm truck and wondered why it backed all the way to the back of the hayfield! Then the two lights got bigger and brighter, though there was no beam. As soon as we saw them rise up into the air, we knew it wasn't our friends in any farm truck.…We sat in front of her house and looked up at the lights for about a minute, when they just "poof" went out, or the thing sped away.

A 1965 case in Augusta County, which fits Hynek's CE-III criteria, garnered much attention and found its way into a book titled *UFOs: A New Look* published by the National Investigations Committee on Aerial Phenomena (NICAP). Waynesboro resident William Blackburn was working at the Augusta County Archery Club off U.S. 250, when he spotted two objects in the sky. According to NICAP:

One of these UFOs, the smaller of the two, descended to the ground and landed approximately 18 yards from the witness. From it emerged three beings of extraordinary appearance, each about three feet high. They were dressed in clothes of the same shiny, peculiar color as the object. One had an extremely long finger on one hand. The beings' eyes were particularly penetrating: according to the witness, "they seemed to look through you." As the creatures approached the witness, to with-in 12 yards, he froze in fright, a double-edged axe in his hand. After uttering some unintelligible sounds, the beings turned and reentered the object through a door that appeared to "mold itself into the ship." The object then ascended and disappeared.

Blackburn's encounter was published in local newspapers. As a result, he received a visit from two strangers who worked for a government agency. They instructed Blackburn not to discuss his encounter any further. Were these the dreaded Men in Black of UFO lore?

The databases of UFO organizations are full of reports from the mountains of Virginia. It is shocking how often anomalous lights are spotted in the night sky and strange craft are seen in daylight hours, and how many folks claim to have had some sort of contact with extraterrestrial beings—up to and including abduction experiences.

Where are these crafts and entities coming from? Are we being visited by explorers from another star system? Or, are these travelers interdimensional? Does the answer to the phenomenon lie somewhere within our own minds—something that cannot be explained until we attain a higher level of consciousness? Most of these questions cannot be answered at this time, although some think they know where the aliens are coming from: underground.

12

A VAST UNDERWORLD

Deep below the surface of the Earth, the voices said, was a system of vast caverns. Artificially made caverns, inhabited by a race of people almost as ancient as the Earth itself, but a people mad and degenerate, a people left behind on a dying earth when the last rocket had left, eons before, for the stars. This race of people was not at all nice to know. They had a habit of feeding upon human flesh.
—*Gray Barker,* They Knew Too Much about Flying Saucers

Caves have long held a prominent role in the world of the unexplained and have occupied the deepest recesses of our imaginations. Perhaps that is why some think that UFOs and their occupants are coming from deep inside the earth. These theoretical subterreanean beings access our world through openings at the poles, underwater tunnels and hidden passages inside of mountains. There is much speculation among conspiracy theorists and UFO buffs that these entities have established a network of underground bases, and from these remote, hidden locations, they are gaining access to the surface world and our skies. If true, it might get even worse—our government may have knowledge of these facilities and is hiding it from the public. Worse yet, some fear the government is working in concert with the subterrestrials, perhaps giving them unfettered access to our planet in exchange for advanced weapons and surveillance and biological technologies. Of course, the powers behind this scheme have no plans of developing these technologies for the good of humanity. Instead, a select group of wealthy industrialists, world leaders, blue-blood families, high-ranking secret society members and the like are hoarding these technologies for themselves. They have acquired advanced medicine and anti-aging products and have even developed a secret space program specifically for themselves and their cronies. Of course, evidence is lacking to substantiate any of these claims, but then again, any conspiracy worth its salt cannot be proven, now can it? Secretive underground government facilities such as Mount Weather in Bluemont, Virginia; Warrenton Training Center in Fauquier and Culpeper Counties; Raven Rock Mountain Complex in Pennsylvania; and the Cheyenne Mountain Complex in Colorado fan the flames, making the conspiracy theories burn hotter.

Long before the idea of a shadow government working in conjunction with menacing subterrestrials entered the public psyche, the pulp science fiction magazine *Amazing Stories* introduced the world to the "Shaver Mystery" in the 1940s. This was a tale of a prehistoric race of sinister beings dwelling inside the earth in cave cities. These evil cave dwellers, called deros—short for "detrimental robots" due to their robotic behavior—kidnap and torture surface people and delight in the misfortune of humankind.

The late Mac Tonnies, a forward-thinking author and researcher of unexplained phenomena, believed that something might be hiding deep inside the earth, but not extraterrestrials. Instead, the beings Tonnies envisioned were terrestrial in nature, and he dubbed them "cryptoterrestrials" in his posthumously published book *The Cryptoterrestrials: A Meditation on Indigenous Humanoids and Aliens Among Us.* According to Tonnies, the cryptoterrestrials are technologically more advanced than humans, but not by a lot. They are secretive and hide themselves deep inside the earth. They also conceal their agenda and disguise themselves as extraterrestrials or beings found in occult writings. Said Tonnies in his book: "Caverns and tunnels repeatedly crop up in the alien contact literature. Witnesses sometimes describe lavish below-ground installations teeming with beings that may or may not be related to humans. This is certainly compatible with the idea that our 'visitors' have been here at least as long as recorded history, spared the toxic excesses of known civilization.

"In effect, they could inhabit an immense fallout shelter, having foreseen our own demise and taken elaborate precautions."

Perhaps as frightening—maybe more so—as the rumors of cryptoterrestrials and extraterrestrials occupying bases underground, are the age-old tales of fierce troglodytes. These stories have long been with us, and, until fairly recent times, involved isolated and backward cave-dwelling people attacking unsuspecting passersby and retreating into their underground lairs.

Many horror films have featured a variation of this plotline, including *The Hills Have Eyes* franchise and, more recently, *Bone Tomahawk*. The fictional movie accounts and the legends certainly have at least some basis in real life. The renowned British explorer Percy Fawcett wrote of a much-feared tribe of troglodytes in the remote jungles of South America in the 1920s. Local Indian tribes and settlers in the far reaches of the jungle greatly feared these cave dwellers.

Occult literature is filled with tales of a worldwide cavern system, part of an overall "Hollow Earth." In some stories, the caverns are inhabited by hundreds of thousands of advanced people led by the "King of the World." This legendary figurehead rules from somewhere beneath the Gobi Desert and is powerful enough to influence political events on the surface world.

In popular culture, the independent paranormal documentary series *Hellier* has featured Kentucky's underworld, and the crew investigated goblins and mysterious beings and their connection to Mammoth Cave, the longest cave system in the world. Mammoth Cave made headlines in July 2019 when news outlets reported that National Park Service officials responded to an incident involving gunfire after an alleged Bigfoot sighting. Some have theorized that Bigfoot creatures spend the bulk of their time in caves. If true, this might explain why a verified Bigfoot carcass has never been found in the woods.

In recent months, nearly every paranormal-themed Facebook page and Facebook group has featured an image of clusters of missing people from the *Missing 411* book series by David Paulides alongside an illustration showing the locations of various cavern systems throughout the United States. The inference is obvious—areas with high concentrations of strange disappearances are also home to vast networks of caves. A thick band running along western Virginia and spilling over into West Virginia and Kentucky is part of the gloomy graphic. Is someone—or something—snatching unsuspecting people and then retreating back into the underworld?

If so, this bodes badly for Virginia, with its more than four thousand caves. A vast network of caves runs underneath the mountains in the western portion of the state. These were formed when rainwater soaked through the soil, becoming acidic, and ate away and dissolved calcium carbonate, the predominant mineral in the limestone bedrock. This created massive voids and cavernous networks.

There are currently eight commercially operated show caves in Virginia: Luray Caverns, one of the most popular caverns in the eastern United States; Dixie Caverns near Salem; Grand Caverns, near Grottoes; Skyline

An illustration of Augusta County's Natural Chimneys, also called Cyclopean Towers, published in the 1872 book *Picturesque America or the Land We Live In*. The chimneys once lay beneath an inland sea, and a cave is located at the base of the formation. *Internet Archive.*

Caverns in Front Royal; Endless Caverns near New Market; the Caverns at Natural Bridge; Shenandoah Caverns near Quicksburg; and Gap Caverns in the Cumberland Gap National Historic Park in Lee County.

To give an idea of just how vast the Virginia underworld is, there are over eighty cave systems in the commonwealth with more than one mile of passage. The Omega System in Wise County is the longest in Virginia, stretching over twenty-nine miles. The Omega System is also the deepest, reaching a depth of 1,263 feet. Eight of Virginia's caves reach 500 or more feet in depth.

GHOST STORIES AND TRAGIC TALES FROM BENEATH THE EARTH

Most anyone who sets foot in a cave will admit, even if they do so reluctantly, that there is a certain eerie feeling about the world beneath our feet. The oppressive darkness, the cool and damp air, the otherworldly landscape and the sense of mystery leave one with the unshakeable feeling that they just do not belong. Many caves in Virginia, however, take it a step further and have their own creepy histories and unsettling tales.

The Caverns at Natural Bridge is such a place. According to legend, shortly after the discovery of the caverns in 1889, a group of men received a dollar a day to explore the underground passageways. After weeks of exploration, the crew found a pit that seemed bottomless. The men dropped objects into the hole to try to get an idea of its depth but never heard them strike the floor. Suddenly, the groans and cries of a woman rose from the pit. The noises grew so loud that the team left the cave in fear. After the incident, the crew ceased its exploration work.

Skeptics would argue that air circulation through the passages of the caverns produced the sounds—they were nothing more than a naturally occurring phenomenon, not the cries of a ghostly woman. That may be. But try to tell that to someone standing at the edge of an abyss while exploring a dank, dark cave!

Grand Caverns, formerly known as Weyer's Cave, has been in operation as a show cave since 1806, making it the longest-running show cave in the nation. The cave walls bear the names of both Confederate and Union soldiers who visited the caverns during the Civil War. While camped near Port Republic, Confederate general Stonewall Jackson allowed his men to visit the caverns to take their minds off the horrors of the war for a short time. Perhaps the bedraggled and war-weary young men left a little something of themselves behind in the caves, something more than their names on the limestone walls. Maybe they left their energy. Orbs and flashing lights are common in the caverns, as are strange unexplained noises.

Gap Cave, once called Cudjo's Cave, in the Cumberland Gap National Historic Park, also bears graffiti on the walls left by Union and Confederate soldiers. The cave is allegedly haunted by a runaway slave. Confederate deserters and looters—miscreants of the worst kind—found the man hiding in the cave and fired a shotgun blast into his abdomen. The callous reprobates left the man to die an agonizing death alone in the pitch darkness.

A Confederate officer—a large-framed man with a straggly, unkempt beard—is the most notable ghost in Gap Cave. He walks back and forth, and unsuspecting visitors have spotted him sitting on the stairs that lead to the bottom of the cave. The old hollow-eyed Confederate has put quite a scare into those unlucky enough to catch a glimpse of him.

In Botetourt County, the property of Dan and Marian McConnell holds a mysterious pit known as the Catawba "Murder Hole." The infamous hole is 100 feet wide and 120 feet deep with a lower level that plunges to a depth of 234 feet. The pit and world below it have claimed cattle and humans, and some believe it hides Thomas J. Beale's legendary loot.

Reminiscent of the tragic heroine Juliet, legend holds that a local woman threw herself into the pit and died after her parents refused to accept the man she loved. Another story tells of Confederate soldiers who caught a deserter and threw him down the hole to his death. There is a legend of a local farmer who killed a traveling salesman and disposed of his body, and the horse he rode, in the Murder Hole.

Of course, there is no way to verify these old stories. They may or may not be true, or they may contain bits of truth. There is a tragic story, however, that can be verified. Twenty-six-year-old David Spencer fell to his death in the Murder Hole in 1958 after his rope broke. Sadly, the fibers in his hemp rope absorbed the chemicals from a spilled cleaning agent while it was in storage, and the rope became weak and unraveled, sending the young man to an early grave.

Many folks have been rescued from the cave over the years after becoming trapped. This includes a dozen Boy Scouts who fell down a slope in November 1958 and a nineteen-year-old girl who fell and broke her pelvis in the late 1960s.

What is it about the underworld that draws us and beckons us to explore? Why are we so quick to ignore the inherent dangers and disregard the plethora of frightening stories? What might be lurking in the vast cave systems spanning Virginia's western edge?

Whether underground or on the surface world, or even in the skies above, Virginia's mountains are full of intrigue, undiscovered creatures, a hidden history and more. For those with an open mind, an adventurous spirit and a sense of wonder, these hills may hold the key to our most perplexing puzzles. Maybe it will be here that a savvy researcher finally proves the existence of Bigfoot or that mountain lions have reclaimed their former range. Someday, a piece of lost history that confirms pre-Columbian contact between the Old and New Worlds might be found on a hilltop in southwestern Virginia. Perhaps a truth-seeking investigator will discover alien bases deep in Virginia's caves. And who knows, a treasure hunter just might hit it big and unearth the legendary Beale treasure. Anything is possible in Virginia's Mountains.

SELECT BIBLIOGRAPHY

Books

Barden, Thomas, E. *Virginia Folk Legends.* Charlottesville: University Press of Virginia, 1991.

Barker, Gray. *They Knew Too Much about Flying Saucers.* New York: University Books, 1956.

Benzaquén, Adriana S. *Encounters with Wild Children: Temptation and Disappointment in the Study of Human Nature.* Montreal: McGill-Queen's University Press, 2006.

Clayton, Lawrence A., Vernon J. Knight and Edward C. Moore. *The De Soto Chronicles: The Expedition of Hernando De Soto to North America in 1539–1543.* Tuscaloosa: University of Alabama Press, 1993.

Dewhurst, Richard J. *The Ancient Giants Who Ruled America: The Missing Skeletons and the Great Smithsonian Cover-up.* Rochester, VT: Bear & Company, 2014.

Eberhart, George M. *Mysterious Creatures: A Guide to Cryptozoology.* Santa Barbara, CA: ABC-Clio, 2002.

Gordon, Danny B., and Paul Dellinger. *Don't Look Up: The Real Story Behind the Virginia UFO Sightings.* Madison, NC: Empire Publishing, 1988.

Hamilton, Ross. *A Tradition of Giants: The Elite Social Hierarchy of American Prehistory.* N.p.: self-published, 2007.

Kennedy, N. Brent, and Robyn Vaughan Kennedy. *The Melungeons: The Resurrection of a Proud People: An Untold Story of Ethnic Cleansing in America.* Macon, GA: Mercer University Press, 1997.

Kercheval, Samuel. *A History of the Valley of Virginia*. Winchester, VA: Samuel
    H. Davis, 1833.
Keyhoe, Donald E., and Gordon I.R. Lore Jr. *UFOs: A New Look*. Washington,
    DC: NICAP, 1969.
Lambert, Darwin. *The Undying Past of Shenandoah National Park*. Lanham, MD:
    Roberts Rinehart Publishers, 2001.
Matyas, Stephen M. *Beale Treasure Story: The Hoax Theory Deflated*. Haymarket,
    VA: self-published, 2011.
McConnell, Marian. *Murder Hole: Catawba Murder Hole Cave*. Huntsville, AL:
    National Speleological Society, 2012.
Schlosser, S.E. *Spooky Virginia: Tales of Hauntings, Strange Happenings, and Other
    Local Lore*. Guilford, CT: Globe Pequot Press, 2010.
Taylor, L.B., Jr. *Haunted Virginia: Ghosts and Strange Phenomena of the Old
    Dominion*. Mechanicsburg, PA: Stackpole Books, 2009.
———. *Monsters of Virginia: Mysterious Creatures in the Old Dominion*.
    Mechanicsburg, PA: Stackpole Books, 2012.
Tennis, Joe. *Haunts of Virginia's Blue Ridge Highlands*. Charleston, SC: The
    History Press, 2010.
Tonnies, Mac. *Cryptoterrestrials: A Meditation on Indigenous Humanoids and the
    Aliens Among Us*. New York: Anomalist Books, 2010.
Vieira, Jim, Hugh Newman, and Ross Hamilton. *Giants on Record: America's
    Hidden History, Secrets in the Mounds and the Smithsonian Files*. Glastonbury,
    Somerset, UK: Avalon Rising Publications, 2015.
Wayland, John W. *A History of Shenandoah County, Virginia*. Strasburg, VA:
    Shenandoah Publishing House, 1927.
Whitcomb, Jonathan David. *Searching for Ropens and Finding God*. N.p.: self-
    published, 2014.
White, David Gordon. *Myths of the Dog-Man*. Chicago: University of Chicago
    Press, 1991.

Articles

Alexandria Gazette. "The Belled Buzzard Killed." March 2, 1887.
Arment, Chad. "Virginia Devil Monkey Reports," *North American BioFortean
    Review* 2, no. 1 (2000).
Bee (Danville, VA). "'Belled Buzzard' Found at Last." April 28, 1931.
Herrick, R.F. "The Black Dog of the Blue Ridge." *Journal of American Folklore*
    20 (1907): 151–52.

Kahn, Chris. "Mystery Surrounds Murder Case." *Indiana Gazette*, October 19, 2003.

Lexington Gazette. "Condensed News." May 23, 1906.

Los Angeles Times. "14 Feared Killed in Virginia Plane Crash: Commuter Airliner Hits Side of Mountain; No Survivors Found." September 24, 1985.

Lutze, Earle. "National Parks Taking Prominent Role in Educational Work." *Richmond Times-Dispatch*, February 17, 1926.

Mroueh, Youssef. "Precolumbian Muslims in the Americas." Paper presented at the Preparatory Committee for International Festivals to celebrate the millennium of the Muslims arrival to the Americas (996–1996 CE), 1996.

News Leader (Staunton, VA). "Alleged UFO Sighters Blame Military." October 25, 1987.

New York Times. "Indian Graves Yield Shenandoah Relics." June 8, 1924.

Nickell, Joe. "Discovered: The Secret of Beale's Treasure." *Virginia Magazine of History and Biography* 90, no. 3 (1982): 310–24.

Old Dominion Sun (Staunton, VA). "Belled Buzzard Again." February 14, 1902.

Petersburg Index. "The Wild Man—What Is He?" April 29, 1871.

Philips, Bud. "A Bigfoot Sighted Near Bristol Began a Reign of Terror." *Bristol Herald Courier*, March 3, 2013.

Richmond Times-Dispatch. "Virginian Sings National Anthem to Protest Eviction." October 4, 1935.

Riechmann, Deb. "Seeking the Key That Unlocks a Buried Treasure." *Washington Post*, September 3, 1992.

Roanoke Times. "Shenandoah Park Body Found; Man Missing 2 Months." October 28, 1996.

Staunton Spectator. "Wonderful Discovery." December 25, 1866.

Times and Democrat (Orangeburg, SC). "News Items." April 2, 1885.

Washington Post. "Family of Five Found Dead in Va. Plane Crash." August 25, 1994.

———. "Largest Skull Ever Recorded Is Discovered by Archaeologist in Stafford County, Virginia." June 4, 1937.

Websites

"Ask A Ranger. Violence Is Nothing New to the Blue Ridge Parkway." National Parks Traveler, May 30, 2010. Accessed January 20, 2020. https://www.nationalparkstraveler.org.

Augenstein, Neal. "Medical Examiner: Missing Fairfax Co. Firefighter Killed Herself." WTOP, April 23, 2016. Accessed January 16, 2020. https://wtop.com.

Austin, Hanna. "Lignite: A Botetourt Ghost Town." *Fincastle Herald*, January 23, 2018. Accessed December 30, 2019. https://fincastleherald.com.

"The Beale Papers." National Security Agency. Accessed January 22, 2020. https://www.nsa.gov.

Blanford, Donald F. "The Ghost of Cudjo's Cave." *The Mountain Laurel: The Journal of Mountain Life*, July 1986. Accessed February 11, 2020. http://www.mtnlaurel.com.

"Bodies of 12-Year-Old Virginia Girl, Grandmother Whose Disappearances Triggered Amber Alert Found." FOX 5 DC, September 6, 2018. Accessed January 16, 2020. https://www.fox5dc.com.

Budryk, Nathan. "Search, Rescue Missions Increasing in National Park." *Northern Virginia Daily*, June 28, 2016. Accessed January 19, 2020. https://www.nvdaily.com.

"Burial Mounds in Virginia." Virginia Places. Accessed December 31, 2019. http://www.virginiaplaces.org.

Champion, Allison Brophy. "Dept. of Game & Inland Fisheries: No Mountain Lions in Virginia." *Culpeper Star-Exponent*, October 3, 2017. Accessed December 14, 2019. https://www.starexponent.com.

Chaplin, Barbara J. Cougar Quest—Virginia. Accessed December 17, 2019. http://www.btcent.com/CougarQuest.htm.

"Corbin Cabin." Potomac Appalachian Trail Club. Accessed January 2, 2020. https://www.patc.net.

"Could Goochland's 'Devil Monkey' Mystery Be Solved?" *Richmond Times-Dispatch*, July 17, 2014. Accessed December 7, 2019. https://www.richmond.com.

Cryptozoology News. Accessed February 17, 2020. https://cryptozoologynews.com.

"Cultural History," George Washington & Jefferson National Forests—United States Department of Agriculture Forest Service. Accessed January 5, 2020, https://www.fs.usda.gov.

Daly, Kyle. "Lost Town of Lignite." *Blue Ridge Outdoors*, January 26, 2012. Accessed December 24, 2019. https://blueridgeoutdoors.com.

Dean, Eddie. "Appalachian Trail of Tears." *Washington City Paper*, February 28, 1997. Accessed October 2, 2019. https://www.washingtoncitypaper.com.

Dinan, Kim. "A Murder in the Woods: The Mystery behind Shenandoah National Park's Last Homicide." *Blue Ridge Outdoors*, March 1, 2018. Accessed January 15, 2020. https://blueridgeoutdoors.com.

Dunkel, Tom. "Lightning Strikes: A Man Hit Seven Times." *Washington Post*, August 15, 2013. Accessed January 19, 2020. https://www.washingtonpost.com.

Frazier, Bart. "The Eminent-Domain Origin of Shenandoah National Park." Future of Freedom Foundation, September 1, 2006. Accessed February 15, 2020. https://www.fff.org.

"Frequently Asked Questions." Melungeon Heritage. Accessed March 13, 2020. http://melungeon.org.

"Geographic Database of Bigfoot/Sasquatch Reports & Sightings." Bigfoot Field Researchers Organization. Accessed February 16, 2020. http://www.bfro.net.

Goochland County Devil Monkey Official Sightings Blog. Accessed December 7, 2019. https://goochlanddevilmonkey.wordpress.com.

Green, Simon. "Texas Becomes UFO Hotspot with '100s' of Sightings Including Snake-Like Objects." *Daily Star*, December 6, 2019. Accessed December 16, 2019. https://www.dailystar.co.uk.

"The Gruesome Truth behind Those Murders on America's Famous Appalachian Hiking Trail." Mpora, October 30, 2015. Accessed January 17, 2020. https://mpora.com.

"A Guide to the Papers of the Low Moor Iron Company." University of Virginia Library, 2010. Accessed December 31, 2019. https://ead.lib.virginia.edu.

Ingles, Laura. "Are Mountain Lions Back in the Blue Ridge?" *Blue Ridge Outdoors*, September 26, 2016. Accessed December 14, 2019. https://www.blueridgeoutdoors.com.

"I Think I Saw Dogman Last Night." Reddit. Accessed January 15, 2020. https://www.reddit.com.

Kyle, Robert. "The Dark Side of Skyline Drive." *Washington Post*, October 17, 1993. Accessed January 8, 2020. https://www.washingtonpost.com.

Lam, Kristen. "Murder Case Where Man Thought Victim Was a Werewolf Ends in Mistrial." *USA Today*, March 29, 2019. Accessed January 12, 2020. https://www.usatoday.com.

Lamb, Elizabeth. "Paranormal Activity in the Caverns." WHSV, June 26, 2012. Accessed February 11, 2020. https://www.whsv.com.

"Mountain Lions in Virginia Reports (June 2017–April 2018)." *Old Dominion Wildlife*, May 2, 2018. Accessed December 14, 2019. http://www.olddominionwildlife.com.

Moyer, Traci. "Body Found in National Park." *News Leader*, May 7, 2016. Accessed January 16, 2020. https://www.newsleader.com.

"National UFO Reporting Center Report Index by State/Province." National UFO Reporting Center. Accessed August 24, 2018. http://www.nuforc.org.

Nicole, Ashley. "The Murders of Julianne Williams & Lollie Winans." Medium, June 18, 2019. Accessed January 20, 2020. https://medium.com.

"Park Service: Wreck on Virginia's Skyline Drive Was Suicide." *Daily Progress*, June 8, 2011. Accessed January 19, 2020. https://www.dailyprogress.com.

Parsons, Shireen. "VA's Iron Furnaces Sparked History of Forest Abuse." Appalachian Voices, April 1, 2001. Accessed January 5, 2020. http://appvoices.org.

"Pound Virginia Werewolf or Was It the Kentucky Dogman?" Reddit. Accessed January 16, 2020. https://www.reddit.com.

"Shenandoah National Park: FBI Asking for Help in 20 Year Old Double Murder Case." *Blue Ridge Life Magazine*, June 1, 2016. Accessed January 16, 2020. https://www.blueridgelife.com.

"Sightings in Virginia." Virginia Chapter of the North American Dogman Project. Accessed January 16, 2020. http://www.vadogmanresearch.com.

"Spooky Creature Creeping Around Va. Neighborhood." NBC 4 Washington, October 19, 2001. Accessed January 16, 2020. https://www.nbcwashington.com.

Strickler, Lon. "Scary Bigfoot Incident in Shenandoah National Park" Phantoms and Monsters, June 13, 2019. Accessed December 23, 2019. http://phantomsandmonsters.com.

———. "Sheep Squatch: Gaining Fame." Phantoms and Monsters, May 20, 2014. Accessed December 23, 2019. http://phantomsandmonsters.com.

"Students Unearth Town's History." *Daily Press*, April 7, 1999. Accessed December 31, 2019. https://www.dailypress.com.

Tharoor, Ishaan. "Muslims Discovered America before Columbus, Claims Turkey's Erdogan." *Washington Post*, November 15, 2014. Accessed February 22, 2020. https://www.washingtonpost.com/.

Thornton, Richard. "Native Americans of the Shenandoah Valley." Access Genealogy. Accessed December 18, 2019. https://accessgenealogy.com.

"Track UFOs." MUFON. Accessed February 8, 2020. https://www.mufon.com.

"Virginia's Mysterious Devil Monkey Sightings." *Appalachian Magazine*, April 27, 2017. Accessed December 7, 2019. http://appalachianmagazine.com.

Wayland, Tobias. "Sheepsquatch." Singular Fortean Society, February 17, 2018. Accessed January 14, 2020. https://www.singularfortean.com.

Williams, Roger. "Other Sightings of Unidentified Animal Reported." *Southwest Times*, August 30, 2013. Accessed February 18, 2020. https://www.southwesttimes.com.

———. "Unidentified Animal Spotted This Week." *Southwest Times*, September 9, 2013. Accessed February 18, 2020. https://www.southwesttimes.com.

"Woodbooger Sanctuary." Norton, Virginia. Accessed December 17, 2019. https://www.nortonva.gov.

"Wytheville UFO Sightings." Unsolved Mysteries. Accessed January 21, 2020. https://unsolved.com.

ABOUT THE AUTHOR

Denver Michaels is an author with a passion for cryptozoology, the paranormal, lost civilizations, ancient history and all things unexplained. In 2016, the Virginia native released his first book, *People Are Seeing Something*, which makes a case for the existence of lake monsters in the United States and Canada. Since then, he has gone on to author *Giants: Men of Renown*, *Wild & Wonderful (and Paranormal) West Virginia*, and several other books covering cryptozoology and paranormal subject matter.

Michaels and his wife sold their home in the spring of 2020 and now travel the country full-time in an RV. Michaels enjoys the outdoors, hiking, fishing, investigating the unexplained and working on new writing projects.

Visit us at
www.historypress.com